Deeper Water

Deeper Water

✦

A Fictional Memoir

Michael W. Boyd

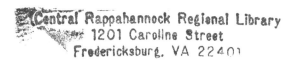
iUniverse, Inc.
New York Lincoln Shanghai

Deeper Water
A Fictional Memoir

iUniverse books may be ordered through booksellers or by contacting:

iUniverse
2021 Pine Lake Road, Suite 100
Lincoln, NE 68512
www.iuniverse.com
1-800-Authors (1-800-288-4677)

The views expressed in this work are solely those of the author and do not necessarily reflect the views of the publisher, and the publisher hereby disclaims any responsibility for them.

All names have been changed to protect the innocent

ISBN-13: 978-0-595-42192-3 (pbk)
ISBN-13: 978-0-595-86530-7 (ebk)
ISBN-10: 0-595-42192-X (pbk)
ISBN-10: 0-595-86530-5 (ebk)

Printed in the United States of America

To Melissa with love

"O Columbia, the gem of the ocean,
The home of the brave and the free,"
            —Thomas A Becket "Columbia, the Gem of the Ocean"

"We'll hoist a hand
Becalmed
Upon a troubled sea …
We'll hoist a hand
Or drown
Amidst a stormy sea."
                —Keith Reid "The Wreck of the Hesperus"

Contents

1

Lightning flashes like quicksilver on the Maryland side sending thunder rumbling across the broad, dark back of the river, reaching the Virginia side of the Potomac with a sudden boom that echoes along its banks on this blustery late October night in 1978 at Columbia Beach. It is a night fit only for eagles—the Columbia Beach Eagles—and their faithful. With each thunderous explosion, however, my mind can't keep from turning to our upcoming season finale for all the marbles with the fearsome Model School for the Deaf and their infernal bass drum booming out the snap count on their sideline. But that's another night and another stadium. Tonight we host the Trinity Episcopal Black Knights from Richmond, Virginia.

All week long the coaching staff has been asking itself, "How can we make a non-conference game against a weak opponent like the Black Knights meaningful?" The answer is simple, just inject trouble with a capital "T" into the mix—Trouble in the form of inclement weather that forces football practice into the gym, a breeding ground for horseplay; Trouble in the form of a head coach who has no patience with aggravation; and Trouble in the form of a star player returning from suspension with a sore ankle and a sore head.

The rain pours down on the Beach Monday and Tuesday, pushing us indoors where once again the battle of Us versus Them is joined. On our side, the scant forces of the coaching staff engage in a thankless campaign to try to convince our players that this week's contest warrants serious consideration and meticulous preparation because, in the final analysis, a season-ending record of 7-1-1 is infinitely better than 6-

2-1. Arrayed against us are the players who are firm in their belief that if they merely toss their jock straps onto the field before the game, Trinity Episcopal will rollover and play dead; that even if Trinity manages to pull off a miracle, 6-2-1 is still a winning record; and if we beat Maret and Model in the final two games of the year, we will win the Tri-State Conference Championship, and nobody will remember the game we played against some private school from Richmond, come win, lose, or draw. So, we are fighting a losing battle, but Jerry Goodson, our head coach, does not give in easily. At least once during Monday's and Tuesday's practices he erupts, quickly dispensing with all blocking dummies and footballs, replacing them with full-court suicides which leave the players' tongues hanging down to their knees and grab-ass a dim memory.

Though not directed solely at him, Jerry's outbursts have their most pernicious effect on our star running back, Flip Richmond. He sprained his ankle three weeks ago against the Hancock Hawks and sat out last week's Quantico game due to some on-the-field antics during the previous week's contest against Riverdale Baptist, but the rest has not helped. In fact, he is limping more noticeably now than when he first injured it. When Jerry has the team run suicides, Flip is the one player unable to go full speed and make the crisp up-and-back cuts required. But in Jerry's eyes, it is Flip who is not being a leader, it is Flip who's not pushing himself, it is Flip who's "doggin' it." So, Jerry does not hesitate to let him have it in front of the team. This verbal whipping, however, does not produce the desired result; Flip doesn't put his tail between his legs for anybody. Instead of speeding up at Jerry's prodding as the rest of the team does, he slows to a walk, punctuated by a slight limp, with his bottom lip pushed out and his eyes glaring at Jerry every step of the way.

"Jerry, his ankle must still be bothering him," I point out.

"It's been three weeks for Chrissake. He needs to stop using that as an excuse (then loudly). All right, Flip, take a blow … (Then in a more conciliatory tone) Let's get some ice on that ankle."

But Flip acts like he doesn't hear him and keeps on walking out his final suicide toward the exit sign at the back of the gym and through the automatic doors, nearly banging them off their hinges with a quick shove.

"Somebody better go find him before he does or says something he'll regret," Jerry directs.

I go because I'm the low man on the totem pole beneath the other two assistants, Whitey and Bear. I search the halls and scan the parking lot through the front door of the school, but no Flip. I finally peek into the training room and find Valerie, one of Doc Chapman's female trainers, applying ice to Flip's right ankle and elevating it. Flip is lying on his back on the training table watching Valerie's every move, an uncharacteristic smile playing across his face.

I begin unsteadily, asking the obvious, "Flip, that ankle still giving you trouble?"

"Yeah," he replies his eyes on Valerie, not me.

"When does it hurt you the most? When you do what on it? It looks to me like you don't have any problem going straight ahead, but when you try to cut, you don't seem to be able to push off it. You don't seem to be able to come out of your cut crisply. Am I right?"

"How'd you know that, Coach?" he says turning away from Valerie to me.

"I've been watching you pretty closely."

"Why?"

"To see if you're well enough to help us on offense."

"Coach told me I was gonna play offense, but he ain't givin' me my chance."

Suddenly, the mask is down and there's animation in his features. "I don't want just a play here and there. I need to carry the ball 25 or 30 times to really get rollin' … Coach, can you put in a good word for me with Goodson? He'll listen to you."

"I don't know about that … I know Coach had planned to use you a lot more on offense in the Quantico game, but with your suspension he had to put that on hold."

"But what about this week, Coach? I'm ready to roll now. I'm ready to carry the mail for ya."

"What about the ankle?"

"Just tape me up, I'm good to go," he says smiling genuinely at me for the first time.

"But you were just limping around the gym, Flip."

"I ain't taped up. I don't never tape when we practice in the gym, Coach."

"Maybe you should."

"Just talk to Goodson for me. I need to tote the leather this week. And when we whip them boys from Trinity, it won't be just because of me it'll be because of you too, Coach Burns."

For the first time, he has addressed by my name. I was beginning to wonder if he knew it.

"All right, I'll try to speak to Coach Goodson about getting you on the field on offense this week."

"Don't just try, Coach. Try hard," he smiles, mimicking one of my pet expressions.

The first time Flip touches the ball out of the I-formation—a toss sweep—he fumbles. The ball bounces right to a Trinity player who returns it 13 yards for a touchdown, putting us seven points down right off the bat. Jerry is ablaze on the sidelines, but he channels his anger into a vigorous bout of handclapping as Flip trots off the field after the extra point with his head down.

"Keep your head up, Flipper. We're going to need you down the road," he yells, slapping him on the butt.

But Flip seems to take no notice of Jerry's entreaty.

Jerry continues to use the I-formation set with Flip at tailback the rest of the first half, but except for an occasional flash, Flip is ineffective, particularly on plays to the outside where he would normally outrun the defenders to the corner or cut back against the grain. His speed is just not there, and he goes down easily on the first hit instead of keeping his legs churning, powering through the tackle, as the old Flip would have done. By the end of the first half, it is still 7-0 Trinity, and he is limping noticeably on his right ankle. There's nothing to do but take him out and go back to our one-back misdirection running attack, mixing in the passing game. At halftime, when Jerry informs the team of this change in strategy, Flip does not take it well. He jerks off his helmet and slams it to the ground. Despite all evidence to the contrary, he still refuses to accept the fact that his ankle is less than 100%.

"Pick it up, son! If you expect to play one second of the second half, you'd better pick up that helmet," Jerry bellows … then softening it a bit, he seethes, "Come on, Flip, we're going to need you this half."

"Yeah, come on, Flip," some of the players echo. Then, others pick up the line and suddenly we're all chanting, "Come on, Flip. Come on, Flip."

Flip stands outside the knot of players who have turned to look at him, hands on hips, face impassive, looking down into the blackness inside his helmet. Slowly, he bends over and picks it up. A cheer goes up from players and coaches alike as if the game were over and we had won.

We kick off to Trinity to begin the second half. Our defense holds them to three and out, forcing a punt. As we line up to receive the punt, I notice we don't have anyone back to return it.

"Where's Flip?" I ask aloud to no one in particular.

"On the bench, Coach."

I hear the thud of the punt and see the ball spiraling toward our goalposts. I watch it hit around our twenty-yard line and bounce dead inside our ten.

"Where's Richmond?" Jerry screams looking around.

"Flip, what are you doing?" I ask as he approaches helmetless.

"Forget about him, Coach Burns," Jerry says, loud enough for Flip to hear him. "He's got his head up his ass!"

"Who you talkin' 'bout, Mothafucker!" Flip explodes as he heads straight for Jerry with his fists balled up at his sides.

Instinctively, I step between them, turning to face Flip, when he catches me with a right cross flush on my left cheekbone. The blow knocks me back a step, but I keep my feet. Immediately, Bear steps between us as Whitey grabs Flip around the waist, hoisting him off the ground.

"Let me down, Mothafucker! Let me go!" He twists and turns in the air like something feral, finally ripping himself free of Whitey's grasp when his feet hit the ground.

Once free, he proceeds to strip down on the sidelines to football pants and a t-shirt. Off comes the jersey. Off come the shoulder pads and the hip pads. Off come the cleats. And the helmet, with an angry heave, is sent flying through the air toward the playing surface, coming to rest in the middle of the field. Flip then takes off at a trot across the Black Knights' end of the field toward the shadows of King Street.

"This belong to one of yours, Coach?" Referee Joe Demetius asks with a trace of a smile on his hawkish face, as he hands Flip's helmet back to Jerry. With sheepishness written all over his face but never at a loss for words, Jerry accepts it, "I guess he kind of lost his head, Joe."

"Just don't lose yours, Coach," Joe reminds him with a wink.

In what remains of the game, somehow we marshal our forces and rally for a victory over the Knights 14-7. After the game, as the four of us coaches gather up the flotsam and jetsam of the contest scattered on the sidelines, we share a nervous chuckle or two over the outrageous exhibition the community has been witness to tonight, each of us wondering silently about the repercussions. All except one, that is. Jerry sidles up to me as we are getting ready to leave and examines the reddish welt on my left cheek, touching it with his index finger to see if I wince. "Maybe you ought to let Doc Chapman have a look at that. It looks like it has some swelling in it."

"It's nothing … I'll put some ice on it when I get home."

"Listen, Burnsie," he says, avoiding my gaze, "Nobody needs to know what was said on this sideline tonight, do they?"

"No, Jerry, no one needs know that."

"Thanks."

Restless from the events of the evening, I drive slowly around the Beach, hoping I run across Flip before heading home. I am not sure what I will say or do if I find him, but I feel I must respond to what took place on the sidelines tonight. I drive back and forth through the Black neighborhood surrounding King Street without seeing a soul, let alone Flip—unusual for a Friday night. About ready to give up my search, I stop at the intersection of 6th Street and King before turning for home. On my left I notice a small ranch painted aquamarine and white. A dark shape is standing in the doorway, framed by the screen door. As I continue to gaze at the form, I suddenly realize it's Flip standing there staring out not saying a word.

"This must be his house," I tell myself. "I should have asked Bear or Whitey where he lived."

I pull over, get out of the car, and approach slowly so as not to spook him.

"Flip, it's Coach Burns. We need to talk."

"Okay. But my Mama's sleepin'. Let's talk outside so's we don't wake her," he says in an evenly measured tone drained of the rage we heard on the sideline earlier tonight. He steps out from behind the screen door.

"Come get in my car. We can talk there and nobody'll see us."

Flip follows me back to the car and slides in on the passenger side, a toothpick hanging from the corner of his mouth.

"Listen, Flip …" I begin, struggling for the right words.

But before I can get started, he says, "Coach I wasn't trying to hit you. I was going after Goodson. You know that, don't you? You know I didn't mean to pop you. You all right, ain't you?"

"Yeah, I'm all right. But right now I'm not worried about myself. I'm more concerned about you."

"You don't need be worryin' about me now. That football shit is over for me. I could never get along with Goodson anyhow. Y'all need to be worryin' about them boys you still got out there, not me. Y'all could still win a championship with what you got out there."

"I agree … I agree with what you're saying. But I think if you came around and apologized to Coach Goodson and the team in front of everybody, he'd take you back in a heartbeat. Of course, I can't guarantee that; I'm not the head coach. I'm just an assistant. But I think I could persuade him to do that."

Silently, Flip stares out the window into the darkness, twizzling the toothpick between his teeth. He seems to be weighing not only the likelihood of Jerry allowing him to return to the team but whether he has enough love for the game left in his heart to stick it out for two more weeks. "Uh … Coach Burns," he says with a look on his face I can only describe as either peace or surrender, "I'm gonna have to pass on this one. I don't mind apologizing to the team, but I ain't never gonna apologize to that honky Goodson. He'll have to win his championship without me. Let's see if he's man enough to do it."

"I'm sorry to hear you say that, Flip. I was hoping there was some way I could help you. That's why I'm out here driving around the Beach in the middle of the night instead of back home in bed."

"Don't worry 'bout it, Coach. I'll be all right. I can take care of myself," he says giving me a soul grip. "But there is one thing you can do for me now."

"What's that?"

"Hook me up with my cousin Fred."

"Where's he live?" I ask turning the key in the ignition.

"Out at the trailers."

"Oh, no," I say turning the engine off, "I'm not hooking you up with any crack, no way."

"Whoa, Coach," he exclaims, flipping the toothpick out the open window beside him, "Who said anything about crack? There ain't no crack out there that I know 'bout. Now cousin Fred might have a bottle of wine with him, but I ain't drivin' so it's okay, see. And since I'm no longer in trainin', I can have me a little nip for the pain, can't I? And if I have a few too many nips, I can always crash in Freddy's trailer. So be a brother and ride me out there. I ain't got no car and it's on your way home, ain't it?"

"I can't do it."

"Come on, Coach … Well, if I have to walk it, I'll walk it," he shrugs, climbing out of the car and setting off up 6th Street.

I start the car and crawl along beside him for half a minute. Then I roll down the passenger side window and tell him, "Get in. I'll run you by Fred's."

"You the man, Coach. You the man," Flip says, hopping back in.

When I stop in front of Fred's dilapidated trailer, he jumps out and scampers up the steps to the door, flashing me the peace sign before he disappears inside. I return the gesture but he's gone by then. I don't know it yet, but this is the last time I will see Flip Richmond for a long, long time.

When the following week slips by and Flip is conspicuous by his absence, I finally approach Jerry on the subject: "What's the story on Flip? Has anybody seen him?"

"He's been returned to the juvenile facility in Hanover County," Jerry explains matter-of-factly. "His behavior on the sideline during the Trinity Episcopal game and the fact that he hasn't shown his face at school this week are both violations of his probation. Law enforcement caught up with him out at the trailer park midweek and transported him to Hanover to serve out the remainder of his sentence." Then with a crooked smile spreading across his face, he adds, "So I wouldn't be looking for young Flip any time soon. He's played his last game for Columbia Beach."

In the years that follow, unless someone else brings him up first, I never hear Jerry mention Flip again.

2

If one draws a straight line on a map of Virginia directly east from Fredericksburg to the muddy banks of the Potomac River, he will find himself on a triangular piece of land jutting into the water like an eagle's aerie high in the blue sky. This is Columbia Beach—home to grizzled retirees, inveterate gamblers, ankle-deep swampers, died-in-the-wool watermen, unregenerate hippies, drunken bikers, poor blacks, crack heads, down-on-their-luck drifters, and the Eagles—the Columbia Beach Eagles.

I am driving east on a two-lane section of Route 3 as it winds its way through what is termed the Northern Neck of Virginia, heading for "The Beach." The sweat pours from my back on this humid July day in 1978, making my seersucker shirt stick to me like a bit of bad advice. When I had mentioned to Dale Reed, one of the assistant football coaches on the Mary Washington High School staff, that I was interested in leaving Fredericksburg for greener pastures, he suggested I contact Jerry Goodson at Columbia Beach High School. He had heard through the grapevine that Jerry was looking for an assistant football coach. So, here I am heading for "The Paradise on the Potomac" on a sweltering day in the middle of July in my '65 VW station wagon—nicknamed "the Blue Bunny" by my old knock-around buddy, Frankie Sherman, for its color and for the number of "hare"-raising adventures we'd experienced in it in high school and beyond, but not for its speed, for in truth, it is as slow as a sea turtle—with no air conditioning.

When I cross Route 301, leaving behind the rolling hills of Stafford and King George Counties, the land begins to flatten like the brown waters of the Potomac it circumscribes. Among the corn and soybean and tobacco fields alongside the road stands an occasional house, but I see no signs of life until I reach Potomac Beach, just two miles outside of Columbia Beach, where the road swoops down nearly level with the river. Here, two seafood restaurants—the Dancing Crab and William-son's—perch next to each other on a little spit of shoreline, sharing a few cars. To the east, the Potomac stretches across the horizon a mile or two—distances being hard to judge on water—to the Maryland side, offering a splendid view for customers enjoying the local fare. But even though it is close to lunchtime, I can't afford to stop; I am running a little late for my interview.

About half a mile farther down the road as I pass River View Acres on my left, I observe a puzzling scene originating from a small trailer park on my right. As I approach it, a short, muscular black man tears out of the trailer closest to the highway and sprints up the side of the road in the opposite direction from town as though someone or something is chasing him. Mesmerized by the sight, I nearly "buy" the ditch beside the road as the figure streaks past me without a stitch of clothing on—he is stark naked.

While everyone else in Westmoreland County is wilting under the heat of the midday sun, inside the main office of Columbia Beach High School, under the influence of 13,000 BTUs of frigid air, in a crested blue blazer and a crisp white blouse, sits the school secretary, Annie Washington, a black woman.

"I'm Michael Burns. I'm here for my 11:30 interview with Coach Goodson. I know I'm running a little late," I say still shaken by what I have witnessed on my way into town.

"That's okay, Mr. Burns. Coach Goodson is waiting downstairs in his office for you. Just take a right out of the office, go down the stairs at the end of the hall, take a left at the bottom of the steps through the cafeteria, his office is the second door on the right."

"Second door on the right?"

"Yes."

"Thanks for your help, Ms. Washington."

"Good luck with your interview."

"Will Mr. Weiss, the principal, be involved in the interview also?"

"Mr. Weiss is no longer with us, Coach Burns. We're kind of between principals right now, but I know they plan on hiring somebody real soon," she says shifting her gaze back to her typewriter.

Cardboard boxes, the kind you get from the grocery store, are stacked everywhere in Jerry Goodson's office—boxes on chairs, boxes on shelves, boxes on filing cabinets, boxes stacked on top of other boxes—all filled with records relating to athletics. In the midst of this peculiar record-keeping system sits the man himself, eating Nabs and working on a can of Diet Pepsi. Although the boyish sparkle in his brown eyes gives him the seeming confidence of a quarterback, the sturdiness of his stocky frame reveals his true nature—he's a fanny kickin' fullback.

"Coach Burns, you didn't have any trouble finding us, did you?" he asks rising from his chair wearing a blue and white UNC baseball hat and extending a soft, fleshy hand.

"I'm sorry I'm a little late, but I've never been down this way before and I got to admiring the countryside on the ride down. This is a beautiful area."

"I'm glad you like it. Some take to it and others don't. For my money, there's no place like Columbia Beach anywhere in Virginia. I grew up here and I've been here most of my life. 'Course, my Momma and Daddy raised me here. They've never left, so there was no reason for me to go either," he says before launching into an interview that rambles on for the better part of two hours (including a tour of the athletic facilities) and ends with the offer of a job, which I readily accept.

"I look forward to working with you, Coach Goodson," I say extending my hand across his desk.

"Glad to have you on board," he replies, returning my grip.

"Oh, one other thing before I forget ... you won't believe what I witnessed on my way into town this morning."

"Where?"

"Out on 205 just past the housing development on the left there. As I was driving along, I noticed this black kid come running out of one of the trailers off to the right. He sprinted up the side of the road past me heading out of town. But what knocked me for a loop, Coach, was that he wasn't wearing a single stitch of clothing."

"He was naked?" Jerry asks shifting forward in his seat.

"Totally!"

"What did he look like?"

"He was about 5'6" or 5'7", light-skinned, broad-shouldered, with kind of a box haircut."

"Did he have a scar on his neck? Could you tell?"

"I'm not sure ... everything happened so fast. He might have, now that I think about it."

"That sounds like Flip Richmond."

"How can you tell?"

"The scar and the fact that he's the only one crazy enough to do something like that."

"Who is he, Coach?"

"He was our starting quarterback for a good part of last season. He's got a cannon for an arm; he can throw the ball 50 yards in the air with a flick of his wrist. But with Flip, if there's trouble out there, he'll find it. Last spring, we discovered someone had been getting into the school at night and vandalizing it. At first, we couldn't figure out how they were getting in because there were no windows broken or doors jimmied. Finally, we realized that whoever was slipping in must have gotten a hold of a master key to the school. That's when we came to the conclusion that Flip was behind it."

"How?"

"Well, a key belonging to Donny Little, the assistant principal, had disappeared right around the time Flip had been sent up to Mr. Little's office on a discipline referral back in February. At that time, Mr. Little didn't think too much about it, but then you'll discover after you've been here a while that Mr. Little doesn't think too much about anything other than chowing down at one of the local seafood restaurants. Anyhow, Little couldn't remember where he'd had the key last—at work or at home. But what came to light later was that while Flip was pleading his case, Little was called to the cafeteria to break up a fight. Instead of sending Flip back to class or, better still, taking him with him, he left Flip in his office. This gave Flip the opportunity to rifle his desk and find the key. It was right around then that the vandalizing began. And it involved some pretty strange shit, too!"

"How so?"

"On one occasion, Flip had tried to break into my office, but he couldn't have known that the master key doesn't work on my door; it requires a separate key. So, he left me a little calling card."

"A calling card?"

"Yeah … a huge turd on the floor in front of my door."

"That is some strange shit," I say with mock gravity that quickly turns to laughter infecting both of us.

"Once the police got him down to the station and strip-searched him, they found the key in his shoe. So we pressed charges against him and Judge Ricks sent him to the juvenile facility at Hanover for four months. I believe he was released last week … Let me make one quick call, Coach Burns. Stick around," he says as he motions me to keep my seat. After a brief conversation he hangs up.

"That was Chief Hurley. They've already got him in custody. It seems you weren't the only one to spot him wearing his birthday suit. Somebody else called the police. They found him out on 205 dressed just the way you described him … or maybe I should say, 'undressed.'"

"But why was he running up the road naked, Coach? Did the Chief say?"

"Apparently, he had been back in the trailers smokin' crack with his buddies when he went crazy, tore off all his clothes, and ran out of the trailer screaming that something was crawlin' all over his skin."

"Will crack do that to you, Coach?"

"I don't know, Coach Burns, I've never tried it … and I don't plan to start now," Jerry states without cracking a smile.

3

So I bid goodbye to the gritty sidewalks of the city in that summer of 1978 and say hello to the tide lapping softly on the shore, the rhythmic "Boom, Boom, Bam, Bam; Boom, Boom, Bam, Bam" of fists striking thigh pads, the collision of shoulder pads crackling like lightning in the evening air, and the sight of shooting stars streaking across the night sky leaving silver trails high above the Potomac River. These welcoming signs signal a fresh start so full of possibility that I drive to Fredericksburg one day before football practice and have a t-shirt made that reads, "The Beach Is a Peach." The players love it.

Halfway through practice one scorching August afternoon, I notice the rotund form of Donny Little making a beeline for me across the dusty expanse of Eagle Athletic Park. He has spent the summer serving as acting principal until a new one can be hired to replace the departed Roger Weiss. But the closer it gets to the beginning of school without a new principal in place the more nervous Donny becomes, given the realization that he might have to fill Weiss's shoes if the School Board can't settle on someone from outside the system. As assistant principal, Donny is in charge of discipline at the high school, but a good indicator of his effectiveness as an administrator is the nickname that some faculty members have hung on him—Donny "As Little as Possible" Little.

"Coach Burns, do you have a minute?"

"Sure, we're going to water break in just a sec."

The horn sounds. Jerry yells, "Okay, Knuckleheads, take a blow."

"What's up, Mr. Little?"

"I see where you have some experience working as a librarian."

"Yes, a little."

"Your resume tells me you worked half-time in the library at Benson High School in North Carolina."

"I was half-time English and half-time librarian, but I'm not certified in Library Science. The principal just stuck me in there because they needed an assistant football coach, and those were the only academic positions he had open. How can I help?" I say beginning to sense where this conversation is leading.

"Well, we've had a bit of a shock today. Ms. Pincus, the lady who works as Lucille Free's assistant in the Media Center, resigned."

"Why?"

"She just walked in this morning and said she was tired of the job. She said she'd been the assistant librarian for 12 years, and she wanted to spend more time with her family. Her father has cancer, you know," he says in a hushed tone.

"No, I hadn't heard that."

"Yes, it's a sad situation … anyway, Dr. Roberson asked me this morning to begin looking for a replacement for Ms. Pincus. I was wondering if, considering your background, you might be interested in the position. I thought I'd give you first crack at it since you're already on staff," he says looking at me with a grin that says he expects me to say "yes."

"I appreciate the offer, Mr. Little, I really do. I enjoyed my time in the library at Benson," I say evenly while mentally salivating at the prospect of not having to do any schoolwork at night after football practice. I couldn't ask for a more inviting offer.

"Good! With her resigning so close to the beginning of school, this really helps us out, Coach. Now all we have to do is find an English teacher to fill your slot. That should be a lot easier than trying to find a librarian at this late date … By the way, if you decide to stay in the Media Center, you'll have to start taking courses towards certification. If I'm not mistaken, I believe Virginia Commonwealth (VCU) offers certification in Library Science. You might want to look into it once football season is over. Also, check with Ms. Free in the library tomorrow; she'll get you squared away on what she expects of you."

Little do I suspect that Lucy Free will do precisely that.

After practice, Jerry is eager to know why Donny Little has come all the way out to the practice field since, according to Jerry, he does nothing but sit on his ass all day long. When I give him the news about Mary Pincus leaving and how they're going to fill the position, he just shakes his head and says, "Well, then it must be true."

"What?" I ask.

"The scuttlebutt is that 'Library Mary' was caught 'dorking' one of the members of the academic team at the Alpha Club Convention this spring."

"You're kidding!"

"No … and with all the rumors flying around this little town, Robo had no choice but to finally confront the student, Kyle Butcher, over it. He admitted it, but from what I've heard, he insisted that Pincus had been the seducer, not him. Whatever the case, Robo had no choice but to ask for her resignation … You know, Burns, it just goes to prove what I've always said."

"What's that?"

"Never put your dick in your job."

"You mean vagina don't you, Coach. Don't put your vagina in your job. Ms. Pincus is a female," I remind him.

"Same difference. It still applies because now you'll be in the library all day long with Lucy Free. And they don't call her 'Loosey Goosey' for nothing."

At 58 years of age, Lucy Free has seen better days, but that hasn't stopped her from continuing to look for them. She has the metallic blonde curls of a latter day Charo and the body of a cheerleader gone to seed. Although she became Head Librarian at Columbia Beach so long ago that her degree in Library Science was on the undergraduate level, it has been rumored that she still has the vivacity to deflower willing male students (not to mention dalliances with male faculty members) at a rate beyond the pale for a woman her age.

With this in mind, I tread softly as I enter the library for the first time that morning in August. Stepping inside, I notice the figure of a woman with her back to me in the Media Center office. She's wearing black high-heels, stockings, a straight black wool skirt, and a white silk blouse. Standing on tiptoe, she's attempting to place a lamp on top of a wooden card catalog.

"Can I help you?" a voice snaps from the yet faceless figure, sounding more like a challenge than a welcome.

"I'm looking for Ms. Free."

"You're in the right place. I'm Ms. Free," she says turning around, showing not a trace of a smile on her face, which bears some resemblance to that of the Medusa. "Who are you?"

"I'm Michael Burns, the new assistant football coach. Mr. Little told me to stop by and see you since I'm going to be working with you in the library this year."

"My God, what'll they think of next! Well, come on in. Welcome," she exclaims extending a hand and breaking the chilliness with a toothy smile that is suddenly bright enough to shame the stars. This is my first inkling of Lucy Free's source of power over the opposite sex, but it is not to be my last.

I sit and listen to Ms. Free expound upon every matter of local interest—what kind of person the next principal should be, whether Mary Pincus has made the right decision, if anyone has a chance against C.A. Goodson in the next mayoral election, what the problems with the school are (and how she'd solve them), what the problems with the library are (and how she couldn't hope to solve them), etc.—with me throwing in an occasional question to keep her talking and me listening for the better part of an hour and a half. What I learn by the end of our conversation is that Lucy Free is someone who knows everything that needs to be known about this one little sliver of the mortal universe perched on the banks of the Potomac River, and she wants to make darn sure that you realize she knows it.

"Did you need any help with that lamp?" I ask when there is finally a break in her monologue.

"Oh, yes, Mike. Could you please? I can get it up on top of the catalog, but with this skirt on I can't bend down low enough to plug it into the outlet."

She stands next to the card catalog, holding the lamp steady with one hand, while I get on my hands and knees, peering into the darkness underneath it for the outlet and the dangling plug.

"It'll be nice to have a man in the library for a change," I hear her declare as I fumble with the plug, trying to insert it in the socket, when suddenly I feel something. Lucy is slowly rubbing her leg along the side of my upper body. Redoubling my effort, I suddenly locate the socket.

"I got it; it's in," I say standing up quickly.

"You did get it, didn't you," she says clicking on the light. "You're going to be such an asset to me here in the library this year. You just let me know if there's anything I can do to help you find your way around Columbia Beach High School. I think you'll find things aren't so bad at this old school," she says as she reaches out, grasps my right hand in both of hers, and nestles it between her breasts long enough to make her message unmistakable.

Later, I find Jerry holed up in the equipment room with another assistant coach, Whitey LeBlanc, rummaging through what appears to be several years worth of football uniforms and equipment in various states of disuse and disrepair. Despite the fact that Jerry has a large upright fan going, it is only exchanging the hotter air in the room for the hot air in the hallway.

"You're just in time, Burnsie. Whitey and I thought you'd never show. Where ya been?"

"Just in time for what? I've just spent the past two hours with Lucy Free."

"Uh, Whitey, do you think they spent all morning straightening books with Dewey Decimal?"

Whitey laughs, shakes his head, but says nothing.

Hal "Whitey" LeBlanc is a stocky man of average height who looks like he lost his way when he left home, his appearance lacking the civilizing influence of a woman's touch. His shape and pallor, reminiscent of the Pillsbury Doughboy, are crowned by an unruly thatch of hair the color of uncooked sweet potato, which sticks out in several directions. And his rumpled attire is often an assemblage of the athletic and the academic for no apparent reason. Today, he's wearing a pair of Columbia blue coaches shorts topped with a thoroughly wrinkled white dress shirt which has one collar point—unbeknownst to Whitey—sticking up at an acute angle. When I reach over to turn it down for him, he jerks back as though I'm taking a poke at him.

"Hey, what are you doin' there, Burns?"

"I'm just trying to fix your collar, for God's sake. It's sticking up."

"Don't worry about it. I'll take care of it," he snaps.

Whitey would be a whole lot easier to get along with if he had someone to help him get dressed in the morning.

"Did you do what I said not to, Burnsie?" Jerry calls out.

Whitey stops laughing long enough to insert into the conversation the astute observation: "I'll bet she was chokin' his chicken, Coach. I'll be willin' to bet she was."

"Save your bettin' for Little Vegas, Whitey," Jerry's tone quickly assuming the hard edge of someone who enjoys authority, "and run up to DW's and bring us back some barbecue plates for lunch … Here's a twenty; that should be enough. Now get outta here," he says with a mock growl, "and tell whoever is working the register to give you a pack of Rolaids. Your breath is startin' to stink."

"Rolaids are for my stomach, not my breath, Coach."

"In your case, it's the same difference," Jerry says as he sends him off with his favorite expression and a few short backhand waves of his left hand.

I wait for Whitey to shove off before I say anything about my morning encounter with "Lucy Goosey."

"What are you doing down here?" I ask.

"Getting ready for the annual CBHS yard sale. Lend a hand," he says motioning for me to jump in.

"Do you make any money on this stuff?" I ask disparagingly.

"Some. Last year we made $380."

"Damnation, that's not too bad."

"It paid for a couple of new helmets and several new pairs of cleats," he says gesturing toward a pile of used red, white, and blue striped football shoes. "Some of our less fortunate players—usually those from the King Street neighborhood—wouldn't be out there practicing with the team unless we were able to provide them with shoes. So, it not only gets the kids out on the field it also helps to get the community involved in the football program. Lets them know the season is around the corner. How did things go this morning with Lucy?"

I recount the details of my conversation with Ms. Free that morning, saving the tale of our carnal encounter over the plug and the socket for last. "That's pretty close to sexual harassment, isn't it?" I conclude.

"Could be. Did you agree to it or did you resist?" Jerry asks with a smile playing around his lips.

"Of course, I didn't agree to it. But it happened so quickly and unexpectedly that I really didn't have time to put up a fight. Besides, I was down on all fours trying to get the plug in when she started rubbing her leg against me. I really wasn't in position to do anything about it."

Jerry goes to the door and looks down the hall in both directions. When he comes back inside, he says, "I'm just making sure Whitey has left. It's probably better if we keep this between ourselves for now. The fewer people that know the better. Mike, if I were you, I'd make a written record of the incident right now, in case it happens again."

"Okay, but ..."

"If it gets to the point that you start thinking about taking it to Dr. Roberson, the more detailed evidence you have the better chance you'll have of forcing him to take action."

"What do you mean by 'forcing him'?"

"Lucy is pretty tight with Robo. He's not going to get too concerned about some first-year teacher at the Beach being the supposed victim of a single incident of sexual harassment by his favorite librarian. But if you go to him with more than one detailed report, you may be able to force his hand."

"But this sort of thing shouldn't be going on. What if it were to involve students?"

"You're right, but so far, assuming that Robo has heard the rumors himself, he hasn't taken any action—direct or indirect—that I know of. I do know, as I mentioned before, that Lucy and Robo have been pretty darn close; but now that I think of it, she's been more than a little friendly with almost every superintendent the school's had for as long as my Daddy's been mayor, which is quite a while. I've even heard tell that she and my Daddy had a thing goin' on back in the '50s, but I've never looked into it too deeply. Know what I mean? I'm a firm believer in the idea that there are some things we're better off not knowing," he says with a wink and a slap on the back.

4

Two games into the season—a 12-12 tie with in-county rival Washington and Lee and a 21-0 loss to Rappahannock—an unanticipated opportunity presents itself: the return of Flip Richmond to the Columbia Beach Eagles.

During the season we routinely meet as a staff on Sunday afternoon—following the Redskins weekly whipping—to watch the videotape of last week's game and formulate a game plan for our next opponent. This activity can drag on for several hours and, depending on the previous week's performance, can produce either a false sense of security (following a win) or excessive cynicism (following a loss). On this particular Sunday, however, despite having fallen to Rappahannock on Friday night, smiles and laughter replace Jerry's usually grim demeanor after a loss.

"Fellas, I've got some news that may shock you, so hold onto your jock straps. I don't know at this point if it's good news or bad news; only time will tell on that. But if we play our cards right, it could make a big difference in how the rest of this football season goes."

"What is it?" Whitey asks. "Have we consolidated with W&L?"

"Have you unearthed another year of eligibility for 'Goose'?" Bear contributes, bringing a smile to Jerry's face.

Goose Jackson is so bright a light in the pantheon of Columbia Beach athletics that he virtually blinds the whole community to any other storied figures. Bennie Payton, James Ralphs, Walter and Gilbert Gaines, and Willis Thomas—all leaders in their own right—have suffered over the years in comparison to Goose. Like many of the Beach's best athletes down through the years, Goose Jackson came out of the relatively small six-square-block black neighborhood clustered on either side of Martin Luther King Street, which lies adjacent to the high school. As Jerry tells it, Goose was one of those athletes who always looked bigger on the playing field than his actual physical dimensions. At 5'11" 165 lbs., his size was not intimidating, but his 10.5 speed in the 100 could send a murmur rippling through the crowd and a chill through the other team's defense every time he touched the ball. He could run around or through a defensive player with equal ease. Essentially, Goose was a AAAA-level triple threat—kicking, running, and passing the football—disguised in the worn uniform of a A-level school.

"No, not quite that good," Jerry laughs. "There'll never be another Goose, but this Eagle might approach him someday. Gentlemen, Flip Richmond will be enrolling at the high school Monday morning."

"You're kidding!" I blurt out, recalling my first and only encounter with Flip.

"No, I wouldn't kid about a thing like this. I talked with Dr. Roberson this morning. He indicated that part of Flip's probation will be attendance in school, and the judge also encouraged Flip's participation in athletics as a way to keep tabs on him on and off the playing field. He feels that a structured environment is Flip's best chance for redemption."

"He might be right, but doesn't that make Flip more our responsibility than the courts?" I point out.

"I agree with you, Burnsie. It's our ball. But I'd rather have him where I can keep my eye on him and he's got a better chance to do something positive than down in Hanover County with the butt pirates, wouldn't you?"

"I concur," Bear says.

"So do I," Whitey chimes in.

"What about it, Mike?"

"I'm sitting on 'Go' as long as he maintains a positive attitude and is helping the team. My only question is what happens if he starts hurting us?"

"We've got to guard against that by keeping everything positive with him. I don't mean cutting him some slack; he's got to abide by the same rules as everyone else. But we do need to be careful about how we enforce the rules when it comes to him. We want to avoid, at all costs, embarrassing him in front of the team. Are we all on the same page with that? We all nod. Good! Now, here's the deal."

"When Flip was picked up in July out on 205 in his birthday suit, he was not arrested—as Jerry tells it—for drug possession, despite the fact that he was higher than the proverbial kite when they slapped the 'cuffs on him. Not only did he not have any drugs on him that day, he didn't have a stitch of clothes on to carry them in. So he was charged with exposing himself in public, not possession of crack cocaine. And it's very fortunate that was the case because possession would have landed him back in Hanover, serving out the rest of his two-year sentence. The public exposure charge was, without a doubt, a violation of his probation, but a minor one compared to being caught with crack. Due to the circumstances surrounding Flip's case—being under 18 years of age and under the influence of drugs at the time—Judge Ricks ordered him to serve 30 days in a rehab center in Fredericksburg. When he completed his sentence there, the court asked that the school step in and allow Flip the opportunity to enroll at the Beach for his senior year and participate in athletics as long as he followed the rules of participation to the letter."

"Jerry, what guarantee do we have that Flip wants to play?" I ask when Jerry finishes.

"I've already talked to Flip. He can't wait to get out there on the practice field. Who wouldn't after being stuck in rehab for the past 30 days?"

"Coach, how are you going to use him?" asks Whitey. "Are you going to play him at quarterback and move Freeman to end?"

"Or running back?" Bear tosses out.

"We can talk about this, but I'm pretty well set in my mind on keeping Freeman at quarterback and using Flip at tailback. Is that what you mean, Bear?"

"No, I meant switching Coleman to running back and using Flip at QB. You know as well as I do he can throw the ball off the lot."

"Yeah, I've considered that, but I don't want to have two players switching positions. Besides, I hate to switch quarterbacks in the middle of the season. You know, the leadership thing and all. Plus, I don't want to put too much pressure on Flip from the get-go."

"With Flip at tailback, it sounds like we'll be running some I-formation. I hate to see us junk our double slot set. That misdirection stuff has got to be difficult for other teams to prepare for," I interject.

"That's a good point, Burnsie. The answer is 'Yes' and 'No.' I am going to put in an I-formation package, which I think will make the best use of Flip's talents. But I'm also going to work him in at Beckner's running back position in the double slot. That way we can run him inside the tackles on the cutback trap and take advantage of his strength. But I'd say, off the top of my head, it'll take him two or three weeks to learn the plays. So we'll spot him a play here and there on offense until he's comfortable. In the meantime, he can help us out right away kicking the ball, returning kicks, and lining up at strong safety on defense, which he played last year.

"The one time I saw him—you know, that day out on 205—he didn't look that big."

"He's around 160 or 165. Wouldn't you say, Whitey?"

"Closer to 150."

"Okay, 150-160, but the bottom line is he's tremendously strong for his size. He never goes down on the first hit. He's not quite in Goose's league when it comes to speed, but he will put a lick on you."

"Remember the hit he put on that big lineman for Manassas Park at the end of the first half last year," Whitey says.

"You mean Lard Bucket?"

"Yeah, Flip hit him so hard in the gut that it not only knocked the air out of him, but two of his own players had to help him off the field."

"And Flip knocked himself out doing it. Mike, Doc Chapman had to crack an amyl nitrate under his nose to wake him up for the second half. If you remember that game, Flip scored twice after halftime to get us the victory while Lard Bucket sat on the bench with his helmet off the entire second half. That ought to tell something about *that* kid's heart, or lack of it. I know one thing about Flip; no one can ever question the size of *his* heart," Jerry states scanning the room for doubters … "Okay, let's take a look at St. Anne's Belfield and see if we can't find a way to get a win this week. We need one in the worst sort of way."

"Mike, don't tell Jerry this, but those two scores he's referring to were the result of the amyl nitrate," Bear jokes.

"Hell, Bear, that's what I call good coaching," Jerry says, throwing a couch pillow in his direction.

5

On the Friday before Labor Day weekend, the last weekend before school begins, an event many of the faculty of CBHS consider the highlight of the school year takes place. This is the annual moonlight cruise across the Potomac aboard the 77-foot luxury vessel, *Lucky Lady*, to Cobb Island for dinner and drinks at Nick's Seafood Restaurant. This excursion offers returning faculty members the opportunity to renew acquaintances with colleagues and to welcome aboard new staff members, like myself. Expectations for this year's cruise are running particularly high because the new principal, Gomer Godfrey, is going to be formally introduced to the faculty that evening. For several of us, this will be our first glimpse of Mr. Godfrey, an older man in his mid 60s, a lifelong educator, and a current member of the Beach's retirement community, whom, Jerry has informed us, Dr. Roberson persuaded to come out of retirement as a compromise candidate when the School Board could not agree on any of the non-residents who interviewed for the position.

At 5:00 P.M., the *Lucky Lady* weighs anchor and sets forth under a cloudless sky and a brilliant sun that turns the dark waters of the Potomac to jewels, dazzling all those faculty members without sunglasses who have sought conversation above deck and sending them on a hasty retreat below deck to the bar tended by a black man of medium height and amiable demeanor. We football coaches, accustomed to the blazing temperatures of a Beach afternoon and sporting our ever present shades, gather ourselves in a circle of chairs on the after deck—Hal "Whitey" LeBlanc, Larry "Bear" Bernoth, Jerry Goodson, and myself—a mighty crew to man the flagship of the Columbia Beach athletic program this year. Slowly, with the application of chilly ones from Jerry's cooler and the carefree undulation of the waves, we begin our round of football stories, each trying to outdo the other, knowing all the while that in the end no one can surpass Jerry, our leader, in either quantity or quality. Stories of players and coaches and games, past and present—nothing goes untold, except what each of us is secretly aching to hear, the true story of what brought each of us to this queer place lying off the beaten path.

After a while, as our storytelling begins to lose a little steam, we are joined by Jonathan Pope, a tall angular man with a full head of dark, puffy hair, who is the current head basketball/baseball coach at the Beach. He is admitted entrance to our fraternity by his agreeable nature and his inability to keep from laughing at our jokes, especially Jerry's. Jonathan's entrance on the scene breaks like a breeze across becalmed waters, filling our sails with a second wind. Reinvigorated, Jerry gets out the weapon for which he is well known among players, coaches, and referees around the Tri-State Conference—the Needle.

"Burns," he begins, "We've got to come up with a nickname for you. We've got 'Whitey' and we've got the 'Bear.' Now all we need is one for you. What 'd they call you up at Mary Washington?"

"Coach Burns," I say without cracking a smile.

"He got you that time, Coach," Bear says high fiving me.

"Loudmouth," Whitey throws out carelessly.

My intensity on the practice field which never lets a good play go unrewarded or a knucklehead play go unnoticed has been rubbing Whitey the wrong way since practices began in August. Finally, it has surfaced.

"You run your mouth just as much as I do, Whitey, if not more; so I wouldn't be pointing the finger at me."

"Aw, don't get your panties in a knot. I was just kidding."

"The hell you were," I yell, standing up out of my deck chair, bringing Whitey to his feet with his barrel chest thrust out.

"Okay, that's enough, you two. Let's not get into a boxing match in the middle of the Potomac River. For Chrissake, this is the moonlight dinner cruise. You're supposed to be having a good time," interjects Bear.

"Right, Larry. Tone it down you two. We're supposed to be thinking up a nickname for Burns. While you're thinking, I'll tell the story of how Whitey got his name," says Jerry changing tack.

"It's no big deal," Whitey immediately protests. "Some of the players found out what my last name means in French (the white) from Mademoiselle Lemonde, the French teacher, so they started calling me 'Whitey.' That's all there is to it."

"That must have been around the same time last year as the Rolaids incident"

"The Rolaids had nothin' to do with it, Jerry. You know that," Whitey protests, his voice rising to nearly a squeal.

"What happened, Mike, was that Whitey got a little nervous before his first game as head JV coach last season. So, when his stomach started acting up before the game, he popped in a couple of Rolaids. They did the trick, but when Whitey here got up to give the team his pre-game pep talk, he got so worked up that he had two little rivers of Rolaids dribbling from the corners of his mouth. Naturally, the players found this more humorous than inspirational and could hardly contain themselves until Bear grabbed a wet towel and wiped his face for him just before kick-off. It didn't help though; the damage had already been done. We got our little hineys whacked by W&L 49-0."

"We would have lost anyway," Whitey offers meekly. "Rolaids or no Rolaids."

"Don't take it so hard, big fella. It was only one game." Jerry says slapping Whitey on the back. "Besides, you got a more colorful name outta the deal, didn't you?"

"How is 'Whitey' more colorful, Jerry?" I cut in with.

"Yeah, Coach, what about it? How can 'white' be colorful?" Bear seconds.

"You guys know what I mean—'Whitey' as in Whitey Herzog."

"He's got white hair; what's colorful about that?" Bear retorts.

"Listen, Buddyroo," Jerry says wagging a friendly finger in Bear's direction, "If you don't lay off, I'm going to reveal the source of your nickname."

Despite Bear's protestations, Jerry proceeds to tell the story of how he received his nickname—it came not from his girth, which is substantial, but from the thick black hair that seems to cover his head, half his face, and just about every inch of his body—from chest to back—and how this was shockingly revealed to the other members of the football staff at the state coaches clinic last summer when the coaching staff saw Larry step out of his clothes for the first time to take a shower.

Despite the group's renewed high spirits, my attention drifts from football stories to the sounds of conversation and soul music filtering up the stairs from the lounge below deck through the late afternoon haze of sunlight and beer. Slipping through the voices below, the strains of The Four Tops' "Ask the Lonely," followed by Harold Melvin and the Blue Notes' "If You Don't Know Me by Now," and then the Cornelius Brothers and Sister Rose's "Too Late to Turn Back Now" waft their way into my consciousness the same way the smell of food cooking on a stove entices a hungry man.

Shaking off my inertia, I push myself up from my chair and step deliberately toward the stairway leading down to the music.

"Hey, Burnsie, bring us some chilly ones when you come back," Jerry shouts after me mistaking my purpose in leaving. "There's only a couple left in the cooler."

"Mike, make mine Miller Lite," yells Bear.

"Same for me," adds Whitey.

I make my way to the head of the stairs without acknowledging their requests. There, I come face to face with an ethereal creature who seems to float up the stairs toward me wearing a broad-brimmed pink sun hat; matching pink clam diggers, revealing a well-turned ankle; and a blue silk shell adorned with white polka dots. As I descend carefully, hugging the starboard side of the steps, she looks up into my eyes, parts her lips in a smile as warm and glorious as the afternoon sun, and says in low voice that is welcoming and seductive, "*Bonjour*, Coach Burns."

"*Bon Voyage*," I respond inanely, uttering the only French phrase that comes to mind at that moment. She continues up the stairs to the deck above without turning her head, leaving me wondering two things: Is this the aforementioned Mademoiselle Lemonde? And if it is, how does she know my name?

In the far corner of the lounge littered with educators, I notice Lucy huddling with Donny Little, Dr. Roberson, and a thin, white-haired man who, I realize after a moment's thought, must be our new principal, Gomer Godfrey. Why else would Lucy be chattering away, her right hand firmly planted in the crook of this elderly man's elbow like a hawk clutching its prey? I raise my hand in a halfhearted wave, but either Lucy sees it and decides to ignore my abortive gesture, or she decides to whisper something in Godfrey's left ear at that precise moment. I can't tell which, but it doesn't matter; she is the last person on earth I want to be seen with tonight anyway. The one person I am looking for, however, is stationed behind the bar loading 45s onto an old-fashioned turntable.

"Hey, man, you've got some bad sounds goin' on tonight," I say, affecting my best Ebonics as I extend my hand to a black man attired in the same black slacks, white dress shirt, and black bow tie worn by the crew members of the *Lucky Lady*.

"Thank you, kind sir," he responds in a voice washed clean of Ebonics, returning my handshake.

"Michael Burns."

"Rondell White ... you're the new football coach, right?"

"Yeah ... I guess there's no sneaking up on anybody around here."

"Things get around this little town mighty quickly. So watch out where you step, if you know what I mean," he warns with a friendly smile.

"I will. Thanks for the advice," then gesturing toward the stacks of 45s surrounding the turntable, "You've got quite a collection here. Are all these yours?"

"Yes," he nods, "I'm not a rich man, but there are a couple of things in this world I find worth investing in—R&B happens to be one of them."

"What's the other?" I ask.

"Videotapes," Rondell answers without elaborating.

"I'm sort of a music collector myself," I say returning the conversation to its original direction. "But I'm more into jazz—you know, Coltrane, Miles, Brubeck, Pharoah Sanders, Lonnie Liston Smith ..."

"Lonnie Liston Smith! I've heard him. That's 'head music', man."

"What do you mean 'head music'?"

"Come on, man, 'head music,' you know," Rondell says with a sly smile curling up one corner of his mouth. "Hey, look for me after the cruise and we'll indulge in some of your 'head music' over at my place ... you're not married, are you?" he calls after me as I head for the coaches table.

6

Ever wonder why coaches, particularly football coaches, always have a separate table set aside for us, and us alone, at social functions? Is it because we can only stand to be with our own kind or because nobody else can stand us? Is it because we only want to talk to each other or because nobody wants to talk to us? Is it because we are afraid of offending others with a careless remark or because others are offended by our mere presence? Or maybe it's something as simple as this—while everyone else is walking around half crocked, we're hanging off the gunnels fully crocked.

As far as tables go, tonight is no different. Our table consists of myself; Jerry and his wife Virginia, the School Board secretary; Whitey LeBlanc; Jonathan Pope and his wife Mary; and Bear Bernoth accompanied by his soon-to-be wife, affectionately dubbed "Pygmy Sally" by Larry due to her short stature, which is accentuated by his large frame. Stealing glances at them, I can't help but wonder what their offspring will look like. While everyone waits for Jerry to make the first move toward the seat of his choice, I boldly claim a chair that backs up to one at an adjacent table, reserved by nothing more than a pink sunhat. "What luck!" I tell myself.

She finally approaches her chair, smiling self-consciously, and sits down behind me without speaking a word. After a few moments, I turn to her, "Ms. Lemonde, how did you know my name back there on the steps?" She turns, fixes me with the most remarkable sea-green eyes I have ever fallen into, smiles a radiant smile encircled by her golden hair, and replies, "Lucy Free mentioned to me that a football coach with curly hair would be taking Ms. Pincus's spot in the library this year. Your hair was the giveaway, Coach Burns. I could have spotted you anywhere with that head of spinach."

"'Spinach.' That's it! That's the nickname we've been looking for, Burns," cackles Jerry, who's been eavesdropping on our conversation from his seat just behind me.

"Thank you, Ms. Lemonde. Guys and gals, Ms. Lemonde has just christened Coach Burns here. From now on he'll be known as 'Spinach'—'Spinach' Burns." Loud laughter and the repetition of my new nickname fill our corner of the room, drawing the rest of the party's attention.

"Coach, *je regrette*. Can you forgive me?" she says reaching out as if to comfort me with a pat on the hand, which I turn into a clumsy handshake.

"Just call me 'Michael.'"

"I'm 'Michelle.'"

"What a coincidence," I remark as I enjoy the momentary warmth of her soft hand. "We have the same first name."

As the lights of Nick's come into view, the ship's wait crew descends upon us like the rapidly approaching darkness bearing away drink orders, salad dressing preferences, and the choice of one of two entrees: Nick's famous Mediterranean chicken or Nick's equally renowned bluefish a la Provencale. These orders are then radioed ahead to expedite the dining process. After fending off a few comments from Whitey concerning my choice of salad—"If you really want spinach with your meal, I'll go back in the kitchen when we land and find it. I'm sure they have some back there, Spinach Man."—I turn back to Michelle.

"Did you order the bluefish?" I ask.

"No, I don't go French on everything, Michael."

"French fries?"

"Too fattening."

"French toast?"

"Yummy."

"French kiss?"

"That's for me to know and you to wonder about," spoken with a playfulness that is belied by a blush rising in her cheeks that beckons to me.

"Let's take a little walk on the dock while we're waiting for our dinners," I suggest.

"Maybe later, silly boy," she says, her cheeks turning rosy again.

"Storm warning! Storm warning! Trouble dead ahead, Matey," Jerry suddenly whispers in my ear.

"What're you talking about?"

"Here comes trouble; there goes romance, Spinach Man," he states aloud, nodding toward Lucy wobbling her way across the lounge toward our table on 5-inch heels with a highball in her hand. Ignoring the wives altogether, she goes straight for the men,

"Hello, fellas. Are y'all coaches having a good time tonight?"

"We'll be doing a lot better once we get some food in our stomachs," Bear informs her. "Lucy, when we dock at Nick's, see if you can get them to put the giddy-up in our orders. I'm dying of hunger … they'll probably listen to you."

"Hear, hear," the others call.

"Now why would they listen to me, Larry? I'm just a poor little old librarian. Get Jerry to go back there and whip those boys into shape. That's what he does on the football field, doesn't he?"

"Yeah, I crack the whip all right; just like you do in the library, Lucy," snaps Jerry.

"That's cool," Lucy observes.

Although I've only been on staff a little more than a month, I've heard Lucy use this expression several times before. And every time I hear her use it I cringe at this signal of hipster approval issuing from the mouth of someone of Lucy's age and position. While I'm busy cringing, Lucy turns to me and says, "Mike, I've been looking for you all evening. There's someone I want you to meet." Flushed with the beer and emboldened by the spirited atmosphere, I decide to have some fun with Lucy for my coaching brethren's benefit.

"Lucy, I've been looking for you too," I say with mock gravity. "I've been wanting to share something with you. After getting to know each other a little better, Michelle and I realize we have so much in common that we've decided to move in together."

"Cool," she replies icily sipping her drink.

"What!" Michelle gasps.

"All right, Spinach Man," issues from the coaches at the table.

"You're a fast worker, Coach Burns, aren't you?" Lucy says, her smile no more than a mask.

"Come on, Lucy, I'm just pulling your leg," I say with a laugh that is not echoed by either woman.

"Don't take it too hard, Lucy," Jerry adds rolling his eyes.

"It's cool," she repeats flatly. "Come on, Coach Burns, I want to introduce you to Mr. Godfrey."

"I'll look for you later," I tell Michelle as I head for the other side of the lounge. When she glances up into my face, there is fury in her green eyes.

After the introductions are initiated, the dignitaries displayed, the welcomes wished, the speeches spoken, the stories spun, the meals masticated, the drinks downed, and the jokes told, it is time to set sail for a night of music and dance on the Potomac under the musical direction of our DJ of the waves, Rondell White. While he spins platter after platter of soul music, I bide my time, nursing a drink, trying to lubricate my courage, anticipating the perfect moment to ask Michelle Lemonde to dance. I wait until I hear the mellow sound of Smokey Robinson's "Ooh, Baby, Baby" to approach her, taking her in my arms at the same moment as I say, "Let's dance."

"No, let's talk," she insists, pulling away, heading outside with me in tow. "Why did you embarrass me earlier?" she says facing me on the outer deck.

"You mean about us living together? I was just joking."

"If that's your idea of a joke, Coach Burns, you're asking the wrong person to dance … I think you should know that," her eyes flashing like knife blades. "You embarrassed me in front of the coaching staff, but if that weren't rude enough, you also did it in front of Lucy—which is even worse. Not only because we're friends but mainly because, dollars to doughnuts, it'll be around the whole town by tomorrow, whether it's true or not."

"All right, all right. It was a dumb thing to say. I admit it. I wasn't trying to hurt your feelings, though. I was just trying to see if I could get Lucy to say 'cool' one more time."

"I don't think that's justification for embarrassing me and hurting my feelings. If you …"

"I'm sorry. I wasn't thinking. I was just showing off for the other coaches … Can you forgive me?"

We're both quiet for an awkward moment—me peering into her face, turned askance. Finally, she utters, "She does use that expression an awful lot, doesn't she?" the storm beginning to blow over.

"I don't want to drive you away now that I've just found you," I say in a voice meant only for her ears.

"I don't want that either," she whispers with a hint of warmth shining in her eyes.

"I'm glad … Let's go back inside and see if we can persuade Rondell to play another slow one," I say taking her hand.

"All right."

Holding her in my arms, I can't help but notice that mademoiselle has my favorite female features: she's nearly my height—five foot nine or ten—with little girl hands, slender arms and soft shoulders, cupcake breasts, a firm waist, shapely legs, and a generous derriere. But it's her aroma that's most enticing—she smells as fresh as flowers on a new day. I pull her close, taking her all in and giving her feet a beating—about which she says nothing—at the same time. Once I slow down and concentrate on where I'm putting my size twelve's we fall into a comfortable rhythm and she whispers in my ear, "That's better."

"Let's go grab a nightcap somewhere after the boat docks," I suggest.

"I wish I could, but I can't tonight. I'm going home and straight to bed. I have to get up at 6:00 a.m. for a French class I'm taking for re-certification down in Richmond tomorrow.

"Damn!"

"Don't worry; we'll get together soon."

"How soon?"

"Call me tomorrow afternoon after I get home and we'll make a plan."

"That sounds promising."

"Here's my number," she says handing me a napkin and kissing me lightly on the cheek. "I should be back by one-thirty or two."

"I still want to find out about French kissing … who better to teach me than a French teacher?" We both laugh.

"Call me," she repeats as she heads across the lounge in Lucy's direction.

I mount the deck flushed with the heady intoxicant of my budding relationship with Michelle and look around for the other coaches. I spy them on the bow deck of the cruiser with wives in tow, scanning the horizon for the lights of Columbia Beach. I saunter their way, saturated with the fullness of the occasion and the warmth of the company I've been welcomed into. I have eaten well on all accounts tonight, and now, unable to indulge in another bite, I look forward to leaning back in a deck chair and digesting it all. But this is not to be, for as none of us realizes, the evening has just begun to serve up additional courses of Columbia Beach excitement.

Jerry turns around beer in hand as I approach. "Lemonde finally turn you loose, Spinach Man?" he cracks looping an arm around my shoulders.

"For the time being," I respond coupled with a playful thump on his swollen belly. The cool breeze off the water and the bow spray on our faces seems to have revived everyone.

"You must have a special talent," interjects Whitey. "Guys have been hitting on her without a prayer ever since I've been here; you come along and sweep her off her feet in one night."

"Yeah, Coach, how'd you do it?" Jonathan Pope pleads. "What's your secret, Big Guy?"

"It must be the hair," I kid shaking my curls. "No, I'm just fooling with you. I guess I just got lucky," quoting the old coach's saw of false humility in the face of recent success. In truth, nothing like this—love at first sight—has ever happened to me before.

Suddenly, Jerry, noticing Donny Little off leash and on deck for the first time this evening, excuses himself remarking, "I'll be right back," and heads straight for him.

Shortly after turning our gaze back to the approaching lights of the Virginia side, we hear raised voices on the aft deck. Bear, Whitey, and I hustle in that direction. Not unexpectedly, we find Jerry and Donny Little jawing at each other—eyeball to eyeball, nose to nose, jowl to jowl—like a baseball coach and an umpire facing off. What they're arguing about so heatedly we're not sure of except that Donny is saying something about Flip Richmond and Jerry is repeating the phrase "as little as possible" while stabbing his index finger in Donny's face. We pull them apart, allow them some finger pointing, let them simmer down a bit, and then send Donny on his way back down the stairs to the lounge followed by Jerry's last words on the matter, "Little, you ain't worth two cents!"

A little later as the *Lucky Lady* nears the Virginia side, the question "Have you seen Lucy lately?" spreads like poison ivy among the teachers sober enough to care. No one can remember seeing her for the better part of the return voyage, and she doesn't seem to be onboard now. Quickly, tipsy educators scour the ship in search of the missing librarian. Finally, a helpful crewmember discovers Lucy beneath the canvas covering of a lifeboat, sleeping curled up with a cabin boy, who is young enough to be her son, not to mention being quite unconscious.

Once Bear and Whitey extricate Lucy, along with her "boat mate," from the lifeboat, offer her a chair to sit down in, and give her a few minutes to recover her composure, she relates a tale to those assembled on deck as dizzying as choppy water on a windy day. According to Lucy, she became so tired on the journey home that she sought a place where she could catch forty winks without being disturbed. So, she climbed inside a lifeboat, nodded off for a while, and then, when she awoke, tried to haul herself back out—to no avail. Soon realizing that she was not going to be able to climb out on her own, she began calling for help. A passing crewmember, hearing her cries, attempted to rescue her from the lifeboat. However, while doing so, he slipped and fell headfirst into the boat, cracking his head on the floorboards, and knocking himself out. Unfortunately, when he fell, he landed squarely on top of Lucy, pinning her to the floorboards until they were finally discovered.

When Lucy utters the final syllable of her story, she slumps down in her chair overwhelmed with exhaustion, inadvertently hiking her dress up above her knees. As pitiable as she appears with her clothes in disarray, her hair in a tangle, and her face more ghastly than I'd ever seen it, there are still two questions that hang in the air like the odor of rotting fish. How did Lucy climb into the lifeboat by herself in the first place? And how had the cabin boy heard Lucy's calls for help when nobody else had? In the end, there are only two people on the boat who can answer these questions—Lucy and the seventeen-year-old crewmember. However, one has said all she is going to say on the subject, and the other is taken to the hospital in Fredericksburg when the vessel docks suffering from a concussion and a loss of memory regarding the ride back from Nick's.

The tide goes out on the night after Lucy's escapade. But as the *Lucky Lady* noses her way deliberately toward the dock, all of a sudden light floods the waters beneath the boat, drawing forth a loud "ah" from the teachers gathered along the deck railing. It quickly dawns on us that the illumination is emanating from the docking lights implanted in the hull of the ship, filling the watery depths with a murky glow. Whitey, Bear, Sally, and I rush down to the aft deck to poke our heads over the gunwale to see what inhabits the waters this close to shore. As we lean over the side, peering into the depths, a shadowy form eight to ten feet long and as big around as a man's arm crosses our field of vision.

"Whoa!" Bear yells, jumping back. "What was that?"

"Catfish," Whitey offers rubbing his hands together as though readying to prepare a meal.

"Nah, I'll eat my underwear if it wasn't an eel," I insist.

"Well, whatever it was, I don't want to be in the water with it," Bear says patting his heart with his hand. "Did you see the size of that thing? That weren't no brim. No, sir."

"Larry, come here and look at this crab," Sally calls from the side of the boat. As she leans over the gunnel pointing out a crab scuttling along the bottom, her keys fall out of her purse and into the water. Fortunately, they are clearly visible in the light brightening the river bottom.

"I'll get them," Bear proclaims gallantly, leaning over the side and reaching into the water … After a few vain attempts to grab the keys, he shouts in frustration, "I can't reach the damn things."

"Be careful, Bear," I yell. "It's deeper than it looks."

"Help me, Whitey. Hold my legs."

Whitey locks Bear's ankles under his armpits, but Bear is a little too large for any one man, let alone Whitey, to hold him inside the boat. So when Bear bends down from the waist trying to reach Sally's keys, he lifts Whitey right off the deck. To avoid being catapulted into the water, Whitey lets go of Bear's ankles, allowing him to splash head first into the Potomac. At once, Sally begins screaming for help while Whitey and I scramble up on the gunwale trying to reach a hand to Bear who's treading water and spitting curses at the same time. As I brace myself, extending a hand toward Bear, Whitey goes flying by me into the drink. Apparently, Sally's temper has gotten the better of her because she climbs up on the gunwale next to me, pointing at Whitey and telling him he has gotten what he deserves for letting go of Bear.

"Guys, watch out for those catfish," I yell as Jerry arrives on the scene just in time to help me pull the two of them out of the drink.

While Whitey and Bear are toweling off, Rondell shows up carrying a leather case full of records in each hand.

"What happened to you two?" he asks.

"We decided to take a moonlight dip," Bear replies sarcastically. "Can't you tell?"

"Yes, I can see that."

Then, Whitey begins relating the incident to Rondell, but when he gets to the part about Bear trying to recover Sally's keys, she interrupts asking Larry if he thought to rescue them while he was in the water.

"Hell, no! That water's deep, for cryin' out loud. My feet didn't even reach the bottom. We'll have to come out here with a net tomorrow and try to scoop them up."

"Oh, Larry, go back in and get them while the boat lights are still on. We'll never be able to see them tomorrow. The keys to the house, the car, my classroom—everything—is on that ring."

"Don't worry; they're not going anywhere. We'll get Whitey's bass boat and scrape the bottom for them tomorrow morning."

While Bear and Sally go round and round, Rondell makes his way with his record cases down the gangplank toward the parking lot. I follow him.

"Can I give you a hand with one of those?"

"Thank you, my brother," he says handing me one. "Listen, why don't you grab some of your 'head music' and drop by my place, if you're not doing anything. It's only 9:30. As they say, the night is still young."

"Sounds like a winner. Let me swing by my house and pick up a few things and I'll be right over. Just tell me how to get to your house."

"Where are you coming from?"

"The Bluff."

"Okay," Rondell says scratching his goatee, "come on down 205 toward town, take a left on 12th Street right past River View; then, take a right on King St. Stay on King Street until you reach the black neighborhood; then, take a left on Washington St. My house is the only house on the left hand side of the street. You can't miss it. You see that piece-of-shit white Toyota," he says pointing to his car. "It'll be parked in front."

I find the house without any problem. Despite meeting for the first time that afternoon on the boat, we quickly establish a comfort zone as if we'd known each other for a while. We proceed to party into the wee hours of the night, partaking of the smoky sacrament of our late-night covenant, listening to my 'head music,' and sampling Rondell's John Holmes video collection—the best I've ever seen.

7

In the days and weeks following my hiring, I discover that Jerry Goodson is the only son of the richest, most powerful man in Columbia Beach, Chester "C.A." Goodson, known for the offshore casinos, election-eve turkeys, "safe" crack houses, and white bucks.

During WWII, C.A. was one of the few able-bodied men left in town who hadn't joined the war effort due to his notoriously flat feet, caused by sesamoid bones in his arches. People around the Beach would remark that the good Lord had always given C.A. a little more than the ordinary citizen. In this instance, they were correct. At any rate, when a military doctor couldn't slip a piece of paper underneath C.A.'s arch during his draft physical, he was classified 4-F. So, he ran for Chief of Police and won, edging a sixty-five-year-old retiree from Baltimore.

But C.A. was just getting started. There wasn't enough crime to disturb a good nap in Columbia Beach during the war, so C.A.'s primary responsibility as Chief was getting all the retirees, particularly those on the riverside of town, to turn off their lights during Civil Defense drills. However, he and his deputy, "Right Handy" Andy Wood, did manage to scare up and capture a lone German frogman coming out of the water at the city beach during one of these drills. As it turned out, the Kraut was a deserter, not a saboteur, who had slipped over the side of a German U-boat that had taken a wrong turn, found itself in the murky waters of the Potomac, and surfaced to reconnoiter. When the German seaman crawled up on shore waving a white handkerchief, "Right Handy" Andy was there to slap on the cuffs while C.A. held a gun (so he wouldn't run) and a flashlight on him (so *The Westmoreland News* could get his picture).

As soon as word got around town that C.A. had captured a Nazi and had him in a cell at the station house, the whole town, including ninety-five-year-old Widow Dreifort leaning on her 63-year-old daughter's arm, gathered at the jail house to get a look at the bewildered Hun. When C.A. finally opened the door to address the crowd, the shouts and cheers could be heard all the way up Main Street to the Beach Gate, where Rte. 205 bends to the right and heads down into the dark recesses of the Northern Neck. To many of these residents, C.A. and Andy had not only gone beyond the call of duty in their contribution to the war effort, but many of them were convinced that the two had risked their lives to save the denizens of Columbia Beach. So, when the war was over and C.A. decided to run for mayor, he was swept into office on the crest of a wave of patriotic fervor.

In the late 40s and early 50s, primarily through the efforts of C.A. Goodson, Columbia Beach realized what could only be described as its golden era. There has never been a time before or since when the Beach served as such a powerful magnet for people and money.

By carefully examining a physical map of Virginia, one will observe that the boundary line of the state extends to the Potomac's western shoreline and no farther. So, technically speaking, someone swimming in the waters off Columbia Beach is actually in Maryland and governed by its laws, not Virginia's. Certainly, there were more than a few residents of the Beach who were aware of this fact at one time or another, but there was only one person with the business sense to put this observation to practical use, turning it into financial gain for the town and himself—that person was C.A. Goodson.

Aware that gambling was legal in the state of Maryland but not in Virginia, C.A. envisioned Columbia Beach as the only town in Virginia offering land access to gambling casinos which nestled like seabirds on pilings that extended out into the Potomac River. So, instead of having to drive thirty or forty miles across the Potomac River Bridge to a club in Maryland to gamble, the citizens of and the visitors to Columbia Beach were able to bang the one-armed bandits while enjoying the recreational and social pastimes offered by the Beach without leaving home, so to speak. Yes, the cash that changed hands in these riverside casinos was taxed in Maryland, but as C.A. was quick to remind you, it was spent in Columbia Beach.

In order to carry out his plan, C.A. had to bring to bear all the power and influence he had accrued since his election as mayor following the war. For in truth, what he was asking the city council to do was change the town's age-old building codes so that a large area of beachfront property could be appropriated for the construction of the casinos. He also knew that this proposal flew in the face of the whole *raison d'etre* of the town, which was to offer tourists the amenities of a beach vacation in a small town setting. Columbia Beach was no Ocean City, Rehoboth, or Myrtle Beach, and it wanted to stay that way.

In the end, it wasn't the renown that attached itself to this sleepy little beach town for engaging in such a bold venture; though, that was part of it. And it wasn't just Chester Arthur Goodson's tremendous popularity and pull with the town's populace; though, that certainly helped the cause. It was the glitter of gold and the prospect of feeding off those who had it for the rest of the residents' lives, and their children's lives, and their children's children's lives, that turned the tide in C.A.'s favor. Although there was grumbling in some quarters that C.A. would be the one who would eventually profit from this seeing how his brother Isaac's construction company was already poised to bid on several beach projects, there was nothing out there, at that point, that was big enough or smelly enough to stop what would change the landscape in Colombia Beach forevermore. So, with all due speed, the zoning regulations were modified, the building codes changed, the contracts drawn up and signed, the kickbacks paid, and the pilings of the first casinos driven, their reflections wavering on the water of the Potomac like dark snakes.

8

In the halcyon days of Colombia Beach as a gambling Mecca—the days of the champagne flights from Washington, DC, in a pink DC-3 to a rickety little airfield outside of town—a pair of white bucks that could have only belonged to C.A. Goodson could be found at almost any time of day padding among the bare feet up and down what remained of the boardwalk, stopping to talk things up or chew the fat or press the flesh with tourists or natives as if there were an election just around the corner. He became a well-known figure on the beachfront to the single secretaries from DC who had come down in pairs by car to soak up the sun by day and canvas the casinos at night, seeking to put some excitement in their lives. C.A. was equally well known to the groups of vital young men with government issue haircuts who pounded their way across the sand tossing a football back and forth or bantering with him in loud voices about who was better—the Redskins or the Colts, the Senators or the Orioles, or the hated Yankees. Underneath all the bravado, he knew they had come here to forget about the war, searching in the casinos at night for the same thing the secretaries sought. He even had words of welcome for the solitary souls who hadn't come of age in time to help fight the war. Now, they lay on the beach smoking cigarettes and drinking beer, gazing out across the Potomac through their dark glasses, waiting for their futures to appear.

For the next two decades, the Beach prospered while the majority of the clientele remained on a social par with most of the town's residents—decidedly middle class. One of the casinos, Whitey's Little Vegas, was well known up and down the East Coast, from Atlantic City to the Carolinas, for its high stakes gambling, its one-armed bandits that paid off large (when they paid off), its swing era dance music churned out on the weekends by Little Jimmy Kennedy and the Vibra-tones, and its late night adult entertainment where the only serious bet-ting was on whose g-string would snap first.

When the tide did turn for the worse in the mid-Seventies, as according to the laws of Nature it will do. When the Potomac turned into an ugly bouillabaisse of crabs, sea nettles, and raw sewage from up river. When the pollution in the Potomac reached such a toxic level that it was barely profitable to be a waterman. When the bikers and the hippies filled the beachfront with their wild antics, driving the bour-geois bettors back across the Potomac River Bridge into Maryland. And when the rednecks and drifters turned the beach itself into their own personal bedrooms and trashcans, sending parents and children back to their hotel rooms. That's when C.A. told himself and anyone else who would listen that all good things must come to an end some time but that the Beach's downward spiral was only temporary. It would bottom out in the near future with the return of classier clientele and a renais-sance would surely occur. However, it would have been closer to the truth for C.A. to admit that the Beach had simply become a victim of its own publicity. Every temptation has its dark side. What drew the mainstream crowds in the first place was the same thing that drew the bikers and the drifters and the loners and the rednecks and the white trash later on—the lure of a big payoff. The problem was that once the riffraff arrived, any tourist with a shred of decency and self-respect hit the road for safer, if not greener, pastures. In the face of this exodus, all C.A. could do was advise the local residents to be patient, let the low lifers spend their money, and avoid patronizing the casinos themselves. When I arrived on the scene in the summer of '78, the beach commu-nity was still operating under that dictum.

With the town's changing fortunes, some believed that C.A.'s popularity was ebbing, and he was ripe for the picking. But that was not the case. Some townspeople insisted it was the hundred or more turkeys he and Jerry hand delivered to the indigent members of the community—black or white, young or old—on the eve of every mayoral election that sewed things up for him. Others spoke of the rumored "safe" crack houses, festering with drug deals in the black neighborhood surrounding King Street, which C.A. had the local authorities turn a blind eye to, insuring him the black vote and swaying the election in his favor. But the surest proof that C.A.s influence was as powerful as ever was when he talked the school board into hiring Jerry to replace the legendary Wayne Barnes, who was retiring as athletic director/head football and basketball coach at the high school.

9

When it came time for Jerry Goodson to matriculate at the University of Maryland, most folks around the Beach concluded that with his better-than-average academic performance and his spotty record on the athletic field he would follow in his Daddy's footsteps and pursue a career in law or politics. But the competitive fires still burned inside Jerry—too brightly some said—so when he graduated from Maryland with a degree in physical education, everybody understood why, except C.A. As Jerry was heard to remark more than once, "There's too much funny business in politics for me."

Unfortunately, despite his intensity—or maybe because of it—he wasn't much of a football coach at first. As a matter of fact, he had either been fired from, failed to have his contract renewed, or left of his own accord every coaching position he had held until he was handed the job at Columbia Beach as a result of C.A.'s arm twisting. By that time, he was so desperate to achieve some success as a coach that he promised himself and C.A. that he'd do any amount of ass kissing required to keep this job.

From time to time, Jerry seemed to take a perverse pride in relating the war stories of his coaching career. Whether it was at a coaches' meeting on Sunday afternoon during the season, driving to a b-ball game over Christmas vacation, or lining the football field on a Friday afternoon before the game that night, Jerry would launch into one of his tales and have us in stitches in no time flat. He seemed to have an almost inexhaustible supply of stories about his run-ins with referees, other coaches, spectators, administrators, and players. I guess he felt that there was no way his past was ever going to catch up with him now that he was under his Daddy's wing. Although his tales were always humorous, if for no other reason than the bitingly sarcastic tone he used in telling them, they had a pathetic undertone as well because he was always the one losing control and doing or saying the wrong thing at the wrong time.

One story he particularly relished telling, probably because he felt he had been more sinned against than sinning in this case, was about the time he was the head football coach at Richard M. Nixon HS on the Maryland side of the Potomac. His mood was dark and growing darker by the minute one evening following a game—his Statesmen had just lost to arch rival John F. Kennedy HS on a last second field goal. To top things off, it had been Nixon's Homecoming. As he strode across the parking lot toward the field house with a glower in his eyes that dared anyone to speak to him, someone dared. A tall, white-haired man in his late 60s or early 70s shouted after him, "You better watch out what you tell the newspaper, Coach." Now, Jerry had little if any idea who the old man was or what he was talking about, but just on the off-chance that the man meant him some harm, he hollered back, "I'm surprised you can read the newspapers," and kept right on walking across the parking lot.

No more than ten seconds elapsed before Jerry felt a bony arm encircle his neck. His first instinct was to try to turn his head up and over to his left to see who was attacking him. He couldn't see the man's face, but he did catch a glimpse of a thatch of white hair. The old man tried to tighten his grip, but Jerry shuffled his feet quickly to the right and behind the man. Then, he reached around the old man's midsection with his left arm, worked his right arm between the old geezer's legs, grabbed a hold of his left arm with his right hand, and viciously jerked his right arm upward into his attacker's crotch. The old man was lifted off the ground and ejected headlong from his headlock on Jerry like a Ferris wheel cut loose from its moorings. He landed face down in the mud beside the concrete walkway leading to the field house. The wrestling maneuver Jerry had used to counter the old man's attack—termed "the grapefruit" in wrestling circles—once again had served him as well as it had during his truncated high school wrestling career.

Immediately, two security officers arrived on the scene and cuffed the old man. One of them had witnessed the attack from across the parking lot, and they both had arrived on the scene just as Jerry escaped from the headlock.

"Do you want to press charges, Coach?" one of the officers asked.

"You're damn right I do. This man assaulted me."

"Yes sir," the other officer said, "we saw the whole thing. You were definitely in the right in defending yourself, sir."

"You're Goddamn right I was. Who is this dickhead anyway? Do you know him? I sure don't," he said pointing at the white-haired man who was now on all fours, struggling to rise to his feet.

"Sir, what's your name?" one of the officers asked the old man.

"He ought to know me," the man said gesturing toward Jerry with a crooked index finger. "I'm Everett Awtry."

On Monday morning, Jerry found out who Everett Awtry was behind closed doors in Principal Homer Phillips' office.

"Everett Awtry," intoned Phillips solemnly, "is Stephen Awtry's grandfather."

"The same Stephen Awtry who's my co-captain?"

"The same."

"But why would he attack me physically? Stephen's one of the best players out there. He never comes off the field … I have nothing but the highest regard for him."

"Well, apparently, Mr. Awtry feels you're heaping too much praise on the black players on the team and not enough on the white ones when you talk to the local paper."

"That's ridiculous! I praise anyone who contributes to us winning on Friday night, regardless of what color his skin is."

"Coach Goodson, Mr. Awtry is not the only member of the community who feels this way. I've already had calls from other parents complaining about the same thing. Now, I'm not sayin' they're right—"

"Of course, it's not right; it stinks of prejudice, Homer, and both you and I know it."

"Jerry, you're probably right, but you can't piss off the entire white community and keep the team from splitting apart right down the middle."

"Well, regardless of what the community thinks, I plan to file assault charges against Mr. Awtry. You can't have parents coming out of the stands and trying to intimidate coaches because they don't like what they read in the paper."

"Oh, I agree … I agree. Now, I can't tell you not to file charges, Coach. That's your prerogative. I'm just warning you that you'll lose Stephen and some of the other white players if you do. Mr. Awtry has already informed me of that. My advice for the two of you is to sit down together and hash this thing out without going anywhere near a courthouse … if for no other reason than the kids. They're the ones who'll suffer if things fall apart."

When Jerry insisted on taking Everett Awtry before the Magistrate, who fined him $25, Stephen and a few of his friends quit the team, which then proceeded to lose all six of its remaining games. So, it was no surprise when contracts came up for renewal in the spring that Jerry was not offered one for the following school year.

10

Ten years ago during the legendary Wayne Barnes' heyday as head football coach at the Beach, there were as many as seven coaches (six assistants plus Wayne) on staff and sixty 60 players on the JV and varsity football teams combined—not too shabby for a A-level program that had to fight for players against the lure of the beach and the money of a summer job on the boardwalk. But Wayne had two things working in his favor when it came to recruiting players: his tireless energy and a sensitive finger on the pulse of life in the community, particularly the student population. During the summer when most teachers were working second jobs or hiding out trying to avoid any contact with students, Wayne was out rounding them up. He recruited them to help run his weekly softball tournaments or to staff his barbecue chicken stands that sold box dinners along Route 205 and Main Street to lighten the wallets and line the stomachs of those weekend visitors to the Beach who often arrived in varying degrees of inebriation. Wayne also made it his business to know everything about every potential Columbia Beach Eagle—what this player was doing, what that one wasn't, who was keeping his nose clean, who wasn't, and most importantly, whose ass he had to kick every now and then and whose ass he had to kiss all the time.

Since Jerry had taken over the program three years ago, the numbers had dwindled to four coaches (including himself) and thirty-five to forty players divided between JV and Varsity. Naturally, with the declining number of players, there was a corresponding drop in the number of victories each year of Jerry's tenure, resulting in a sub-.500

(4-6) record last season for the first time in as long as anyone could remember. The old timers and derelicts who hung on the fence surrounding the playing field on Friday night stated with the certainty of diminished memory that Wayne Barnes had never had a losing season in his twenty-five years as head coach. In the fog of time, they had all apparently overlooked the fact that in Wayne's first year as head coach he finished 1-9 and was almost run out of town on a rudder. Fortunately, he never experienced another losing season in twenty-four years, which is all the community recalled when comparing Jerry to him. In their eyes, Wayne had done no wrong and Jerry could do no right. But Jerry wasn't worried—or if he was, he never showed it—as long as C.A. was still in office.

In reality, Wayne and Jerry were about as far apart on the coaching spectrum as two coaches can be and still be successful. Where Wayne was organized, Jerry is innovative.

Wayne Barnes scripted every minute of every practice, punctuating the beginning and end of each practice period with a screech from an air horn wielded by a ball boy. In addition, Wayne's coaches' meetings in preparation for the upcoming contest began immediately following that Friday night's game, whether win or lose, home or away, often lasting into the wee hours of Saturday morning fueled by pizza provided by the Eagle Booster Club. Jerry, on the other hand, has the reputation of being a coach who can adapt his offense or defense to the talent he has available any given year—an invaluable trait to have if your numbers are down.

If Jerry is blessed with a strong-armed QB, he'll spread the field with a Run and Shoot or a Shotgun approach. If he has a strong running game but no one who can throw the ball, he might implement a direct-snap single wing or double wing offense. If he has neither a bullish runner nor a QB with a rifle arm, he 's completely comfortable employing a misdirection Wing T concept. Every year it's a different offensive or defensive system based on what Jerry considers to be the strengths and weaknesses of the team. He might not be as organized or disciplined as Wayne Barnes, but he has a wide-ranging knowledge of the game which allows him to pull something out of his bag of tricks each year, keeping the Eagles competitive.

When it comes to personality, Wayne had that charisma that drew people to him the way people were drawn to Lombardi and Landry. Though relatively low key on the practice field, among his peers at a softball tournament or coach's clinic, he held court with a booming welcome and a friendly word for almost everyone. And the ones he didn't speak to were invariably the ones who always wanted to have a word or two with him. With apologies to C.A. Goodson, when people up and down the Northern Neck thought of Columbia Beach, they thought of Wayne Barnes first. Perhaps the real measure of his charisma, though, was not only the solid citizens of the Beach who always had a kind word to say about him, but as the song says, "All the bad guys knew him and they left him alone." ("I Get Around" by The Beach Boys) Conversely, Jerry has that white hot intensity that either sets you afire or consumes you. Once he steps on the field, his unbridled energy easily boils over—too easily some say—particularly if he thinks a player or a coach is not putting forth the same effort he expects of himself.

I get my first glimpse of Jerry's volatile nature during an intra-squad scrimmage prior to the opening game of the season. The first team defense under Jerry's tutelage is scrimmaging a second-string offense under my direction. On an off-tackle power play, George Johnson, the left defensive tackle, keeps standing up against a double team by the tight end and offensive tackle, giving ground and opening the hole for the runner. Trying to maneuver around George makes it difficult for the onside linebacker, Bennie Clayton, to slide over and make the tackle in the hole. Jerry instructs George more than once to avoid giving ground against the double team by getting underneath it and working his way to the ground. But George doesn't seem to grasp the concept. He wants to stand up and look for the ball carrier, widening the hole and making it difficult for Bennie to make the tackle. Finally, he calls Bennie over and whispers to him to run right over George the next time it happens, stuffing George back into the off-tackle hole. I run a draw and a sweep before Jerry signals for me to run the off-tackle play at George again. Just as before, George stands up and gives ground against the double team. But this time, Bennie hits George so hard in the back that he drives him and the double team to the ground, tripping up the runner before he can scamper through the hole.

Bennie's inspired play seems to send a jolt of electricity through Jerry, not only because the ball carrier has been stuffed but, more importantly, because Bennie has done exactly as Jerry has directed him to do.

"Atta boy, Bennie. That's the way to do it. Super job, son," Jerry shouts, clapping his hands furiously and pounding Bennie on the back. "You can't play it any better than that! No, sir!" But George, still wincing from the shot in the back Bennie has delivered, takes none too kindly to the praise Jerry heaps on Bennie. He glares at Jerry a moment with his hands on his hips and then says the wrong thing, "That's your favorite boy ain't it, Coach … nigger lover."

At this Jerry goes berserk. He grabs George by the facemask and swings him around in a half circle while we all watch, paralyzed with the fear that he will break his neck. When he finally lets go, players and coaches rush between the two to prevent any further violence. Jerry, realizing he has crossed a line of coaching propriety, backs away.

George tries to come at him, is restrained, curses Jerry, and then begins stripping off his football uniform right there on the practice field. Needless to say, Jerry ends practice early that day.

11

Later that afternoon with the sun sinking like a ship in the western sky, I seek refuge from the ugliness earlier that day by gathering up Michelle and two-dozen steamed crabs from Williamson's and retreating to the wooden picnic table under the elm tree in my backyard. We eat silently at first focusing all our energy on digging enough pieces of crabmeat out of our shells to constitute a meal. Because she is methodical and I am not, it is a task Michelle welcomes and I detest. The events on the practice field still disquiet me, but at first I say nothing, hoping to preserve the industry of the moment and satisfy our hunger as long as possible. This makes Michelle happy and keeps me from having to dredge up the tale of Jerry's antics at practice while we are eating. The crunch of child size wooden mallets cracking open crabs is the only sound to be heard.

Finally, beginning to get frustrated with the victuals, I raise my eyes from the growing pile of broken crabs before us and ask innocently, "How was school today?"

"Fine, just fine. All except Danny Riddle, that little jerk! I had to sit him down after second period and threaten to call his parents."

"Why? What'd he do?"

"Oh, the usual. He wouldn't leave Roxanne Miller alone. Every time she'd answer he'd say 'LeRock' under his breath, trying to get a laugh out of Wally Potts and Christopher Smith."

"I'll bet he had no trouble doing that."

"None whatsoever."

"Which one's Roxanne Miller?"

"You've seen her—the short heavyset girl with the long brown hair parted on the side and the round face."

"Oh yeah, her … what were they calling her? 'Le Rock'? She is a little chunky," I say with a smile beginning to steal across my face.

"It's not funny, Michael. Don't you dare laugh about it. By the end of class, Danny had the other two repeating it with him. Poor Roxanne was in tears. It was deliberate cruelty on their part."

I return to cracking crab claws and digging for crabmeat. "You'll have to admit it is kind of an imaginative nickname," I casually add, only to realize immediately that I have said the wrong thing.

Eyes flashing like pistols, Michelle snaps, "It's not imagination when you hurt somebody's feelings; it's cruelty … pure cruelty! For you to suggest otherwise puts you in the same boat with Danny Riddle. The girl is self-conscious enough about her weight without being ridiculed."

"All right … all right. I was just kidding," I plead trying to extricate myself as quickly as possible from the last thing I need at this moment—an argument with Michelle.

"There's no kidding about a thing like this. The girl was in tears, Michael!"

"Okay, I'm sorry. You're right. I shouldn't have said it. Now let's just drop the whole thing." I bend over the remaining crabs looking for edible prospects.

But Michelle is not quite ready to resume eating. "What's gotten into you today? This is not the Michael Burns I know—taking the bully's side."

"I'm not taking their side, Michelle," I insist, beginning to burn.

"It sure sounds like it … did something happen at practice today?"

I remain silent for a minute nibbling crab readying myself to relive the events of the afternoon practice but unsure of how Michelle will respond. Brushing a strand of blond hair out of her eyes, she glares at me across the table—waiting for me to speak.

"Jerry did get into a bit of a confrontation with George Johnson."

"That's nothing new, is it? From what I've heard, Jerry does that once a practice."

"Yeah, well, that may be true, but this was different. This was a physical confrontation."

"You mean punches were thrown?" she asks, the glare in her eyes softening to puzzlement.

"No, no punches were thrown, but Jerry did have him by the face mask jerking him around. I was afraid for a second that Jerry was going to break his neck. Thank goodness Whitey and Bear and some of the players stepped in and pulled them apart. I've never seen Jerry that hot before. And to tell the truth, it scared me a little. That's why I didn't jump in myself to help stop it."

"I'm glad someone did. What started the whole thing?"

I recount for Michelle what the practice situation had been, what had taken place on the field, and what words had passed between the two that set them off.

When I finish, she asks, "How is he going to wiggle out of this one? He's physically assaulted a player. That's grounds for dismissal, isn't it?"

"Yeah, if the story gets out. But I doubt if any of the coaches will take it up with Dr. Roberson. I know I won't. None of us want to lose our jobs over something that's really Jerry's problem. A few of the players might mention it to their parents tonight, but unless George Johnson goes to his parents and they make a stink about it, I doubt if anything will come of it. In fact, Jerry is probably over at George's house right now apologizing to him and telling how valuable he is to the team. And if he doesn't gather the team around him at the beginning of practice tomorrow and apologize to George in front of everyone, I'll eat my underwear. I wouldn't be one bit surprised if Jerry doesn't try to turn this whole incident into a motivational thing—you know, we've got to pull together as a team to overcome this adversity—that kind of thing. That's the way coaching works, Michelle. Good coaches can turn dog shit into diamonds," I assure her as though I actually believe what I am saying.

"Michael, it's all a bit too violent for me. I don't see that violence within you."

"Oh, it's in there," I insist tapping my chest with my forefinger. "You've got to realize there's a thin line between intensity and violence, particularly in the coaching profession. As a coach, you need to have that intensity about you that your players will buy into and exhibit on the playing field. You just have to keep it from boiling over into physical intimidation like it did inside of Jerry today."

"Yes, it's called self-control. Teachers have to maintain it at all times in the classroom even when they've got a jerk like Danny Riddle plucking their strings all period. Jerry's no different than any other teacher. If he crosses that line between, as you say, intensity and physical abuse, he should be subject to the same rules as we are."

"You're right, Michelle. I can't argue with you. I'm just giving you the reality of the situation—I don't think anything is going to come of this. Once he apologizes things will get back to normal pretty quickly, I think."

For a moment or two, we quietly survey the battlefield in the war between the crabs and us. It appears we have won this battle, but certainly there are more skirmishes, perhaps even, confrontations ahead. We both know that.

"To be honest about it," I say as we begin cleaning up, "Jerry is a lot like someone else I know."

"Who?"

"My old man—always ready with a quip or a joke, quick with the back of his hand or his fist, basically blinded by his own intensity. I never knew when he was going to cross that line and begin using me as a punching bag. But it wasn't just limited to me. He'd come home liquored up from a night on the town with his service buddies, and if my mother said one word to him about it, he'd chase her around the house slapping at her. I never saw my mother, still overweight from a recent childbirth at the time, move so fast. He scared the hell out of me. My brothers and sisters never knew when he'd go off next. I promised myself back then that I would never treat my own family that way, that I'd never resort to violence as a means to an end, but here I am working for a head coach who's intensity can explode in a minute—just like my Dad. Apparently I must be drawn to that kind of person. What do you think?"

"No, you're not like them, Michael. Don't think that for a minute," Michelle says hugging and kissing me tenderly.

"Well, I hope you're right. But if I hang around here long enough, what's going to keep me from following in Jerry's footsteps? You know it's sort of in my blood."

"Me." She laughs, hugging me again.

The next day Jerry gathers the team around him before practice: "Fellas, there's no way around it; I had a bad day yesterday. There's no excuse for losing my temper and acting the way I did. So, I'd like to apologize to George. He's an important member of this team; I hope he'll stick with us. I'd also like to apologize to all of you. I'm supposed to be setting an example, but I sure didn't do that yesterday. There's absolutely no room on the football field for the kind of behavior I exhibited. But, by the same token, I don't ever want to hear the word 'boy' or 'nigger' used by either a player or a coach in referring to Bennie or any other black player on this team. Is that clear, George?" George nods. "Do we all understand each other?" A smattering of "Yeah, Coach." "I can't hear you!" Jerry roars. This time there's a resounding "Yeah, Coach." "Okay, let's go out and have the best practice we've had all year!"

12

We suit up Flip for practice on the Monday prior to the Belfield game, and he immediately makes his presence felt by laying the wood to any younger or smaller player who finds himself in Flip's area during defensive scrimmage. If Flip cannot get in on the tackle from his strong safety position, like a heat-seeking missile, he looks for any unsuspecting offensive player to hit. We come to recognize the "thump" of these hits like a mallet striking a pumpkin, echoing across the practice field. Pretty soon, every offensive player has one eye peeled for Flip when he comes off the ball until the whistle blows ending the play. Despite the fact that these hits border on being cheap shots, we are not inclined to rein him in. The coaching staff, including myself, punctuates each hit with loud approval:

"Good shot, Flip!"

"Way to rock his world, son!"

"That's good football, Flipper!"

"That's a man out there now, fellas!"

Flip's demeanor on the field is a good example of the toughness we want every Columbia Beach Eagle to demonstrate. In fact, he's not blindsiding anyone, not deliberately trying to hurt them, just trying to intimidate anyone he can, except for the few that are stronger and just as tough as he is, like our stellar two-way tackle, James Ralphs, for one. Besides, why would we want to stifle someone who can out hit just about any Eagle who will be suiting up on Friday night?

One impression of Flip grows within me as the week wears on, but rather than mention it to any of the other coaches I keep it to myself. Why—I don't know? Unlike any other high school player I have ever coached, Flip's face remains expressionless after he scores a touchdown or punts one 50 yards or makes a tough catch or completes a bomb on the halfback option or even does something as basic as make a textbook one-on-one tackle. The only time I ever see him raise his hands above his head in celebration is when he "terminates" another player, hitting him so hard that he "pancakes" him, knocking him flat on his back. Jerry has come up with the former label, borrowing it from a Schwarzenegger movie, and by the end of the week the rest of the players are calling Flip "The Terminator." He seems to like it, though, because the corners of his mouth curl up slightly whenever he hears it.

The boys from Belfield go quietly at Eagle Park on Friday night, 21-0. The Saints employ a split-back veer offense which is very predictable because, like most veer teams, they run it in sequence—dive, quarterback keep, option pitch; dive, quarterback keep, option pitch—to the wide side of the field. They also tip the direction of the inside dive by lining up the dive back a little closer to the LOS (line of scrimmage) and leaning him forward on his down hand, while the pitch back is set back a bit with his weight on his heels. We don't know whether the St. Anne's coaching staff does this on purpose or inadvertently, but it's a dead giveaway for which direction the ball's going on almost every play.

Knowing these offensive tendencies, we line Flip up as the strong safety three yards outside and five yards off the tight end or offensive tackle to the wide side of the field. Then, we make it simple for him. When he sees the QB option down the line toward him, we tell him to fly across the LOS like his pants are on fire and bust the chops of the pitch back, whether he's carrying the ball or not. Carrying out this assignment with a vengeance, Flip becomes instrumental in our victory. After getting thumped by Flip a few times, the pitch back begins to take his eye off the pitch and look for him. Midway through the second quarter, he has coughed up the ball twice, both turnovers resulting in touchdowns for us. By the second half, the Belfield quarterback, realizing that Flip is laying in wait on the pitch, quits pitching the ball at all on the option. That's the point in the game when we conclude that the Saints are going to have a long ride back to Charlottesville.

Besides his intimidation on defense and booming punts and kick-offs, Flip also contributes a nifty punt return of 38 yards down to the Saints' 14-yard line that sets up our final score. His inaugural appearance at Eagle Park this season has been a success on all accounts, yet when I pat him on the back and extend my hand after the game in congratulations, he gives me a sidelong stare, a limp handshake, and a curt, "Thanks, Coach," but no smile.

13

There is only one high place on the river between Potomac Beach and Columbia Beach—the Bluff. Rising some forty to fifty feet above the turbid Potomac, it is a fit place for an eagle to nest or for stars to fall from the sky or for a romance to begin. It is where my house is perched and where, after we eat, I can't wait to bring Michelle on our first date.

It's the Saturday night after Labor Day. We're heading back to the Beach from dinner at The Flying Frog, a French restaurant in Fredericksburg recommended by Mlle. Lemonde, snaking our way through the darkness in the Blue Bunny like a phosphorescent eel slithering through the depths. I turn left on Locust Lane and whiz past the cluster of tinderbox houses at the head of the street. When it runs out, I bear left, paralleling the edge of the Bluff for a few yards. Then, I turn left on Mimosa and pull into the driveway of my very own tinderbox on the right. Before we go inside though, I suggest we take a walk on the Bluff under the stars. Michelle slips her hand in mine as we locate the grassy path through the open field between my house and the river, leading us to the edge of the Bluff. We sit down on the very lip of it, dangling our feet out over the river in the moonlight as though falling is the farthest thing from our minds.

"This breeze is wonderful," she exudes.

"Invigorating."

In the moonlight her smile is bewitching, drawing me toward our first kiss, but instead I wait, biding my time, allowing my passion to rise like the tide.

"Have you been teaching French long?"

"I've been teaching it for … this is my sixth year. I started here in 1973."

"And all six have been here at the Beach?"

"Yes, they have," she nods. "Anything wrong with that, Spinach Man?" This is one thing I like about her; she's almost as quick to become playful as I am.

"Watch it now. Watch it," I say with a grin. "I just mean haven't you ever thought about teaching somewhere else? Somewhere where there are more 'cultural opportunities,' so to speak. I'd think that would be important to an intelligent person like you; Columbia Beach doesn't even have a movie theater."

"But it does have a beach."

"Some beach! If the crabs don't get you, the jellyfish will."

"I've thought about leaving now and then, but Fredericksburg is just a half hour up the road, and I can always ride over to the Maryland side."

"Largo, Maryland … that's a real cultural Mecca."

"Actually, I just happen to appreciate the pace of life here at the Beach. Nobody's in too big a hurry, except for you," she says brushing the hair out of her face.

"What do you mean?"

"Oh, you just got here and you're already thinking about leaving."

"No, I'm not."

"Yes, you are. If you were offered a head-coaching job next year, you'd leave here in a heartbeat. Wouldn't you! Wouldn't you!" she says, poking at one side of my rib cage and then the other trying to tickle me.

"Be careful. You'll knock me off this perch and then I won't be going anywhere," I warn her, covering up in mock fear. "Yeah, if the right head coaching job came along, I'd jump at it. But the way the team's been doing so far this season, I doubt if I'll have much to recommend me."

"You've only played three games; don't give up on the team already."

"Oh, I'm not giving up on them …"

"Why not stick around here for a while? Jerry can't do it forever."

"Jerry's not going anywhere," I mumble, then, swinging the spotlight back on her. "So, you'd never leave the Beach?"

"I wouldn't say 'never,' but I really like my job here, and the community—the administration, the students, and the parents—seems to appreciate me. I take my French students to Quebec every March—those that want to go and whose parents can afford it.

It broadens their perspective to visit what is actually a foreign country with a different language and a whole different culture. For some of these kids, it's the first and maybe the last time they'll go beyond Fredericksburg when they talk about 'getting off the Beach' … Hey, that reminds me, I'm always looking for parents and faculty members to go along and help me chaperone. Why don't you think about helping me out this spring?"

"I'd like that. There wouldn't be any conflict with football season, that's for sure. Yeah, I'd love to go to Quebec. It's just like being in France, isn't it? I've heard all they speak up there is French."

"The Quebecois attempt to maintain their cultural integrity by speaking French in most situations, but they do speak English—if they know it—when necessary."

"Let's go in," I suggest, reaching out with a hand to help her up. "That breeze off the water is starting to get a little cool, don't you think?"

When we get back to the house, I pour us each a glass of wine, and we ease down on the floor in front of a blank TV with our backs to the sofa. As the wine overtakes us, both of us understand there is no need for conversation tonight. I turn to her and find her lips with mine. I have never felt lips as soft and as warm as Michelle's. Our tongues entwine and I grow swollen with desire, like a wave gathering itself toward shore. I roll over on top of her. When our hips meet and our genitalia touch, she comes with all the desperate exhilaration of a drowning swimmer breaching the surface for air—again and again and again.

After that first night—a night that doesn't end until the dawn's early light, a night in which not a single minute of romance is sacrificed for sleep—our appetite for each other becomes insatiable. Over the next few weekends, our lovemaking grows so torrid that we actually start avoiding each other during lunchtime at school. I get my lunch early and retire to my desk in the Media Center while Michelle chitchats with Lucy and the other teachers over her lunch tray at the faculty table in the cafeteria. A momentary locking of our eyes or a casual touching of hands across the lunch table might send our thoughts traveling to places they should not go in the middle of the school day. But Michelle's darkest suspicion—one that increases in direct proportion to the heat of our passion—is when we are together, others in the community can somehow sense our carnal chemistry. Michelle is convinced they look at us, knowing why we are rarely, if ever, seen out and about Friday night after the game or on Saturday. Lying on the bed with the covers ripped aside, soothed and spent but still warmed by her passion, I reassure her, "Let them think they know what goes on between us indoors, but they will never know what is going on in our hearts."

14

Our next game against Hancock High School is one of Jerry's scheduling masterstrokes. Needing to fill an open date on the fourth week of the season after Bethlehem Baptist has punted out on us—as Jerry puts it, "Since they'd lost to us last year with the Lord on their side, they probably don't expect anything different this year."—Jerry comes up with an away game against the Hancock Hawks, a team we've never heard of before let alone played against. The only drawback is that Hancock, Maryland, where the mighty Potomac is no more than a stream, is located approximately sixty miles northwest of Washington, DC, five hours by school bus from Columbia Beach.

We discover early in the game that the Hawks, though a willing opponent, lack two ingredients that would increase their competitive potential: size and speed. Lacking neither, we are able to build a 17-0 lead by halftime without any difficulty. Flip returns the Hawks second half kick-off to around midfield, but a block-in-the-back penalty moves the ball back to our eight-yard line. Feeling that the score is decidedly in our favor, Jerry decides to let Flip stay in the game to get some work on offense. This turns out to be a decision he will regret. On Flip's first play from scrimmage, he bolts straight up the middle of the field on the inside trap for 60+ yards before he is dragged down by a Hancock tackler with the angle on him. Unfortunately—we have no inkling of how unfortunate—he sprains his right ankle while being tackled and at Doc Chapman's direction sits out the remainder of the game alternately scowling or grimacing with his right foot propped up on the bench under an ice pack. His run, however, leads to another score and we end up defeating the Hawks, 27-6. Despite our success, the journey home through the dark, unfamiliar Maryland night feels like the longest bus ride known to man, especially for Flip.

15

Michelle and I discover early in our relationship that we are aquatic soul mates. We love water whether it is a mountain lake or the Atlantic Ocean—not that this coincidence is unexpected when it involves two people who have spent most of their lives growing up around it. She went to high school in a little town in Florida—Titusville, which lay just inland from Cape Canaveral, where her father worked as an engineer for NASA. I was born in Ft. Lauderdale, FL, where my old man had served on the city police force during the late 40s and 50s when it was known as "Ft. Liquordale" after the cases of illegal whiskey that were smuggled onto the beaches there. However, I had done most of my growing up on Lake Barcroft in the Northern Virginia area—Arlington and Falls Church—outside of Washington, DC, where my parents still reside.

We have set our sights on exploring the North Carolina beaches in the spring and summer—Nags Head; Emerald Isle; Atlantic Beach; Wrightsville Beach; Ocean Isle; and Sunset Beach, the southern most beach in North Carolina—because lying seven or eight hours down the road from Columbia Beach makes them less than ideal for a weekend getaway during the school year. No matter how much we enjoy the solitude of walking on the beach in winter, we aren't going to spend most of the day and night riding in the car to do it. We settle for a more accessible beach, one once ballyhooed as the "Finest Ocean Beach North of Florida," Virginia Beach. It quickly becomes one of our favorite haunts during the fall and winter for two reasons: It is no more than a three-hour drive from the Beach, so if we leave right after school on

Friday, we can usually get to Virginia Beach by suppertime if the traffic's not too heavy. More importantly, the Queen Anne Hotel on the beachside of Atlantic Avenue possesses the largest—at least a 25-meter kidney—and most uniquely outfitted indoor swimming pool we have ever seen anywhere. If there is one activity we prize even more highly than a walk on the beach in the winter, it is swimming indoors in the Queen Anne's heated pool while streams of water intermittently arch over the pool's surface from four jets placed strategically around its perimeter.

The first time Michelle and I stay at the Queen Anne she is so enthused by the pool and its amenities—including a hot tub and a sauna—she decides to replace her old one-piece bathing suit with a more revealing two-piece. She even ventures out onto the boardwalk to one of the few shops that remain open year-round—the kind of place I have never seen her frequent before or since—and picks out a sky blue bikini. She looks so luscious in it when she first dons it in the store that we must quickly retire to our room to try it on and take it off a couple of more times. Then, we hit the pool for a swim to christen the new aquatic apparel.

16

The game against Riverdale Baptist is always one of the biggest of the season for the Beach, if not for the Samaritans. It is the opportunity for us to challenge a program that requires two luxury rental buses to transport the trainers, coaches, and fifty+ players who dress for the game; a squad that doubles our numbers and outweighs us on average twenty to twenty-five pounds per man upfront; a school that is the reigning Tri-State Conference champion; and a team we have never beaten in the brief history of our rivalry.

"Gentlemen, we don't have the size to match up with Riverdale. All of you are aware of that fact, I'm sure. They have one 260-pound tackle who, their coach informs me, is being recruited by the University of Miami," Jerry begins our Sunday coaches' meeting with. "Nor do we have the numbers to equal theirs; fortunately, the rules only allow each team to play eleven at a time, so we're on equal footing with them there."

"The one advantage we may hold over them this year is speed. Compared to us, they're slower than dog piss. So, I'm convinced we have a solid shot at beating them this year if we can find ways to use our quickness to our advantage on Friday night. One way to capitalize on our edge in quickness, I believe, is to use our one-back formation to spread the Samaritans out all over the field, invite them into some man-to-man coverage situations against the pass, and then take advantage of the match-ups between our receivers and their defensive backs. The skinny post could be very good to us against man coverage, by the way. Also, if we can catch them in man-to-man coverage, we can sprint Coleman out, let him show pass, and then tuck the ball and run while their d-backs are trying to cover our receivers."

"While we're attacking the edges with the pass and the run, we want to be sure to continue to threaten the middle of the defense with our inside trap. Bear, we're going to change up the blocking scheme on the trap this week. Instead of leading on the onside linebacker in their 4-4 defense with our pulling guard, we want to trap the defensive tackle so that we can hit the hole quicker straight up the field with either Flip or Peter."

"That might be a good play for Flip, Coach. He's quicker than Beckner. You saw how he busted that inside trap at Hancock." I throw this out for consideration while Whitey nods his agreement.

"That's what I'm thinking, Burnsie, but we'll have to see how his ankle is this week before we put too much on his shoulders."

"One other thing we could do out of our buck-lateral series," I offer, "is to stretch the second option into a sweep rather than an off-tackle play. All Riverdale has seen, if they've scouted us, is the off-tackle option where we kick out the defensive end with our pulling guard. They haven't seen us run the ball outside the d-end off our inside trap action before."

"Whoa, hold up, Spinach Man, how would you block that?"

"I'd bring our tackle down on the inside linebacker; reach block the defensive end with the tight end or slotback, depending on the formation; and lead on the safety or cornerback with the puller, whoever shows his face first outside the d-end. I'd tell the ball carrier to put his hand on the outside butt cheek of the guard and stay there until he makes his block. Then, make his cut up field off that block."

"Not bad, Burns, not bad at all for a rookie. It'll be another way to attack the edges against them … Let's put it in. Where ya been hiding that one, Spinach?"

"Lucy drew that one up for us in her spare time in the Media Center, Jerry," I deadpan. Whitey and Bear laugh.

"I'll bet she did, Spinach Head. I'll bet you two have been working real close on this." More laughter comes from Whitey and Bear. "If we can execute our game plan on offense and if Flip's ankle will allow him to play and if Burns can milk some more plays out of Free—now we're all laughing—we've got a decent shot of handing the 'Good' Samaritans their jocks on Friday night. And if we do that, we'll be in the hunt for a conference championship, men. Now, let's talk a little defense."

Our defensive game plan works to perfection; we stifle their power running game with our attacking defense and force them to do something they don't do well—pass the football. Our defense hangs a big goose egg on the scoreboard next to where it says "Visitor." The outcome is never in doubt. We score four touchdowns—three in the first half, two via the pass, one a skinny post to Jimmy Roth, the fastest white boy on the field, the other to Flip out of the backfield. We win 28-0 as if beating Riverdale were as easy as eating custard pie.

As we walk off the field victorious, we should be elated at finally accomplishing what has never been done before by any Columbia Beach team—beating Riverdale—but we aren't. All that's left in our cups is the milk of victory that has gone sour. We all wait for Jerry to say something. He does.

"Kind of sucks the Goddamn joy right out of you, doesn't it!"

"You got that right, Coach."

"You ain't lyin'!"

"There's no doubt about it."

We are all referring to a troubling act of poor sportsmanship committed in the waning minutes of the fourth quarter by Flip. He is ejected from the contest, with the outcome already decided, for kicking a Riverdale player in the throat, an action serious enough to warrant the appearance of an ambulance with its lights flashing and EMS personnel on the playing field, an occurrence that is guaranteed to bring a chill to any potential victory celebration.

When Flip gets to the bench, Jerry asks him what happened. He replies that the injured Riverdale player had attempted to injure him by roll blocking his tender right ankle. So, he kicked him in the throat. When Jerry points out to Flip that the game was almost over with the outcome no longer in question, all Flip says is, "He got what he deserved."

Later, sitting around his office, Jerry comes to this conclusion," I've got no choice but to sit him down next week. He's embarrassed the team and he's embarrassed the school."

"Next week is Homecoming, Jerry," Whitey reminds him.

"I know … I know. You think I don't know that, LeBlanc?" Jerry snaps throwing his halfway folded play sheet at Whitey's head. Then, in a voice that's barely audible, he mutters to himself, "I always knew that kid had too much 'nig' in him."

17

By our third trip to Virginia Beach, the mind numbing sameness of I-95 south from Fredericksburg to I-64 east outside of Richmond to bucking the cross-town hustle and bustle of the Tidewater area traffic through Newport News, Hampton, and Norfolk to the refuge of the Queen Anne displeases Michelle. Her philosophy of travel, I discover, is based on a single, inviolable rule—the journey there must be as interesting and entertaining as the destination reached. This seems like a tall order when it comes to the Queen Anne, but undaunted, she fishes the map of Virginia out of the pocket of the car and scours it in search of those less frequented byways which will make our excursion more engaging without sacrificing too much in the way of time.

On one of Michelle's first road adventures, we savor the poignant decay of dying towns along Route 1 running south from Fredericksburg—Massaponax, Thornburg, Arcadia, Cedon, Golansville, Carmel Church—ghosts along a highway time forgot once I-95 sprang to life supplanting it. We stay on Rte. 1 through Richmond and on into downtown Petersburg, where rarely is seen a white face, to the home of the tastiest and most moistful fried chicken we have ever eaten, Church's in the heart of P-burg. We stop for a two-piece snack box each and then proceed through the city until we connect with Highway 460, just south of town. 460 is a four-laner like Rte. 1 but with one difference—it runs through the broad cultivated fields of tobacco and corn in southern Virginia which make it seem wider and more expansive than 1.

One other thing we discover about this part of Virginia—this is hog country. That means barbecue stands and sit-down restaurants dot the highway, all vying like culinary tarts for the dinner dollar of the few drivers who frequent this road. Fortunately, we pick a winner on one of our first trips down. Wright's Barbecue between Waverly and Wakefield offers the spiciest and most succulent vinegar-soaked barbecue, sliced or minced, we've ever eaten, not to mention the size of the portions, which demands that we summon the required take-out box.

An hour south of Wright's we begin wending our way through the early evening, stop-and-go congestion of Suffolk County to I-264 east, which shoots us over and across Portsmouth and downtown Norfolk all the way to Atlantic Avenue by the beach.

Perhaps Michelle's most remarkable itinerary as self-appointed trip navigator is the John Tyler Highway running south from Richmond through the bottomland beside the James River. This thin black line, identified on our roadmap as Rte. 5, is nothing more than a two-lane road that parallels the twists and turns of the river from just below the capital to just above Colonial Williamsburg. Not only does it offer a historic panorama of pre-Revolutionary America—Shirley Plantation (the oldest in America), Fort Pocahontas at Wilson's Wharf, and the Jamestown Settlement—its natural beauty stuns us. Poplar, oak, birch, and elm overhang the road for most of its course, filtering the sunlight into gentle shades of green and dizzying our senses as we roll through bands of shadow and sunlight. Between the trees off to our right, we catch glimpses of the coppery River James. "Does anyone really know that this road exists?" we ask ourselves. There is hardly a single car besides our own on this tiny stretch of road and no signs designating it as a Scenic Highway. Poor John Tyler, first he plays second fiddle to a sickly William Henry Harrison; then, the state of Virginia overlooks the stretch of highway named after him. It's sad, but we're filled with the joy of discovery anyway.

Just outside Williamsburg, we regretfully must turn off Rte. 5 onto Rte. 199, which skirts the city, taking us away from the only working colonial village in the U.S. and Vic's famous seafood restaurant tucked away under the York River Bridge. With the idyllic portion of our drive behind us, we access I-64 east from Rte. 199 and jet along it with a few hundred others to old reliable I-264 and then on to the beach where deeper pleasures await us.

18

I do not know whether it's trying to prepare the team for Friday's game against Quantico amid the distractions of Homecoming week or the situation with Flip, or both, but Jerry is manic the whole week. It isn't that Quantico is a good team—they are mediocre at best this year—but Jerry, with all the distractions, can't keep himself from expecting the worst. So, he scrambles around all week like a cat in kitty litter trying to cover all the crap that's going on.

On Thursday night at the Homecoming bonfire at Eagle Park, the situation with Flip comes to a head. On Monday, Donny Little got the jump on Jerry by making a recommendation to Gomer Godfrey that not only should Flip be barred from Friday's game—as if Jerry hasn't gone far enough in disciplining him—but he should also be prohibited from attending the bonfire and standing on the sidelines with the team during the game. If Donny has his way, Flip will have to watch the game from the stands. Jerry feels that suspending him from playing in the game is sufficient punishment and that he should continue to be treated as a member of the team. Jerry's point is well taken, but Gomer, in light of Flip's legal situation, feels they need to come down on him as hard as possible to let the court know that the situation is under control. All of us agree that it is a touchy situation. If the school comes down on him too hard, he may bolt the team and wind up hanging out back on King Street; on the other hand, if we don't discipline him strictly enough to satisfy the court, Judge Ricks may send him back down to Hanover.

We are standing around the bonfire listening to Jerry share his thoughts for the ninth or tenth time that day on the decision that's been made regarding Flip when Donny Little sidles up, hands in pockets, bearing the proverbial olive branch. It is his to offer freely now since he has gotten his way with Godfrey. Jerry ignores him at first, "If he's going to continue to be a member of the team, then treat him that way. Don't treat him like a complete stranger to the program one week and then welcome him with open arms the next week. You know what I mean. Don't isolate the kid. He screwed up. That's for sure! But isolating him won't do him a bit of good. In fact, it might just drive him away altogether. Don't you agree, Mr. Little," he says turning to face Donny squarely for the first time.

"I didn't come over here to talk about that, Jerry. We've already talked about it enough for one week, haven't we?"

"And you got your way, didn't you," Jerry seethes, his eyes narrowing.

"Jerry, I'm warning" … Donny stops his thoughts in midstream, deciding to pursue a different tack, "I just came over to wish you and the team the best of luck against Quantico tomorrow night," Donny says sticking out his hand while cocking his head to one side. But Jerry won't take it.

"Little, you ain't shit," Jerry spits out as he takes a step toward Donny.

"Hey! What do ya think you're doin'?" Bear asks as he and Whitey step between Jerry's outthrust chest and Donny's ponderous form.

"What's goin' on here?"

"He'd like to see us lose," Jerry growls. "Wouldn't you, Lard Ass?"

"You're wrong, Coach Goodson, dead wrong," Donny shouts retreating toward the safety of the other side of the bonfire.

Suddenly, one of Columbia Beach's finest looms up out of the night, "What's going on here, Coach Goodson? Everything all right?" he asks thrusting his face into Jerry's, checking for the smell of alcohol.

"Yeah, officer, everything's cool now. Nothing to worry about."

"Yes, well, there are students here. You probably ought to watch your language, Coach Goodson," the officer says still looking closely into Jerry's eyes while Jerry tries to avoid his gaze.

"You're right, officer," Jerry says trying to regain his composure. "I think the heat of the fire must have got to me." He laughs halfheartedly. "I'm all right now. Things just got a little hot for a moment, that's all … Whitey, Bear, I appreciate what you just did," he says clapping them both on the back. "I almost did something I shouldn't have. I better go apologize to Mr. Little," he mutters as he strides off in Donny Little 's direction.

Jerry appears more subdued than usual Friday morning when I speak to him in the hall between classes. He's just concluded a meeting with Gomer Godfrey, which included Donny Little, concerning the previous night's fireworks.

"Rough night," he observes flatly, "even rougher morning. We need a win tonight in the worst sort of way." I nod.

"You're right about that, Coach. But don't worry about it. We'll be fine," I respond trying to buck him up as he moves down the hall toward the gym.

By warm-ups that evening, Jerry's motor is revved back up, though, clapping his hands, curling his top lip back over his teeth in a mock snarl of intensity, slapping players on the butt, and pacing back and forth on the sidelines prior to the opening kick-off like a caged animal. As the Marines line up to receive the kick, I'm standing right behind him when I hear him tell the Quantico player nearest him, "You're going to eat a lot of points tonight, son. A whole lot of points!" The Quantico player looks at him for a minute with a blank expression on his face, not knowing what to make of this braggadocio coming from an opposing coach.

Unfortunately, the only team eating any points in the first half is the Eagles. After a listless performance, we are on the short end of a 14-0 score and Jerry is madder than a jellyfish. As a matter of fact, I've never seen him quite this angry before. He's so red in the face from the yelling he's done in the first half at the referees and the players that I fear he'll have a heart attack. When I point out to Bear and Whitey as we jog off the field at halftime that he seems more emotionally involved in this game than any other so far this season, they both concur. And when I mention to him that the team seems a little down and might need some pumping up as the players head for the dirt infield of the baseball diamond behind the east end of the football field, he snaps, "Let me handle this. I'm going to blow it in their ass!"

He begins by drawing a line in the infield dirt with his toe, saying, "All of you with one ball in your sack get on the other side of this line, and those of you with two balls in your sack get over here with me on this side of the line …" The rest of his tirade is lost to me in the blackness between the stars that hover over Eagle Park that night, but the two things I still remember are his final nearly hoarse admonition to the team—"If you're going to go back out there and lose this game, at least go down fighting like men."—and the roar that goes up from the players, along with their raised helmets, as Jerry speaks his final words.

And what are the consequences of Jerry's deviltry, aside from giving him a splitting headache? We score thirty-five unanswered points in the second half, including a final touchdown as the result of Jerry calling for an onside kick, which leads to our thirty-fifth point, after the issue has been decided. When we question him about it after the game, he insists that he wasn't running up the score; he just wanted to put some big numbers up on the scoreboard to please the Homecoming crowd. And, as promised, Quantico rides back to the base with their stomachs full, having eaten well.

19

Despite the fact that I have never seen Michelle shy away from a juicy piece of fried chicken, she has her own set of dietary principles which she adheres to. Some of them I have begun adopting in lieu of my usual "football coach's fare"—steak, beef ribs, hamburgers, pizza, beef barbecue, and bologna sandwiches.

Michelle's Dietary Dictums

1. Begin each morning with a cup of coffee; it will prepare you for anything life brings your way that day. Remember, coffee always goes better with something sweet on the side, so pie for breakfast is A-OK.

2. Avoid red meat like the plague. It will curdle your stomach, clog your arteries, and give you gas. Chicken, seafood, and pork will make you feel good inside.

3. Substituting rice for potatoes and stir-frying your food indicates you have synthesized Eastern and Western cultures in your diet and your worldview. You are truly a Sixties survivor.

4. You can never eat too many vegetables or too much fruit.

5. Never eat anything sweet after 9 p.m. at night.

6. Always drink at least one glass of red wine before going to bed at night.

7. Always eat food when it is steaming hot; never let it cool before consuming.

8. Hollandaise and Bearnaise sauces can make the most tasteless food taste better.

9. When it comes to gastronomical excellence, never substitute bourgeois quantity for aristocratic quality.

10. When visiting our nation's capital, always make a special trip to Aux Fruits de Mer on Wisconsin Avenue for seafood with a French twist.

11. When vacationing in Virginia Beach, head straight for The Jewish Mother delicatessen on Pacific Avenue for omelets, crepes, pitas, soups, sandwiches, and salads.

After shaking the road off our shoulders with a walk on the beach and a quick dip in the pool, we usually throw on some clothes and make our way to The Jewish Mother. Now comes the most enjoyable and, yet, most difficult moment of our sojourn—what to order at "The Mother." Michelle can't decide between the Seafood Omelet Cajun Style or the Beak-n-Brock, a crepe with Mom's famous chicken and broccoli covered with a tart lemony Hollandaise sauce. I am torn between the Seafood Crepe, also smothered in Hollandaise, or the Mother's Mother, Mom's chicken salad, consisting of Mom's famous chicken, apples, raisins, and nuts, along with avocado, Muenster cheese, and mayo between two slices of rye bread. Michelle finally settles on the Seafood Omelet with baby shrimp, crabmeat, and veggies inside, while I step up to the plate and make the out-of-character selection—the Mother's Mother. Why out-of-character? Because the only chicken salad I've ever eaten prior to this point in my life is the kind mixed up with just mayonnaise and some celery thrown in for color. When I savor the Mother's Mother for the first time, I experience a cornucopia of tastes like nothing I've ever experienced before. One bite and I'm hooked for life on this delicacy.

Later that night when we're back at the Queen Anne lying on the bed, still under the salutary influence of our meal, we both agree that the dishes at Mother's are a lot like good sex. "How so?" you might ask. Well, almost every entree on the Mother's menu is crowned with a single common ingredient—Hollandaise sauce—that makes each dish delectable. Good sex, by the same token, also has that one element that makes it special every time we conjugate the verb *to come*—It's the spice of love, true love.

20

I don't know whether it's the closeness of this small water-town community or the fact that the players are only two wins away from a conference championship, or both, but the team, amid all the crap of the past two weeks, pulls itself together like a cornered rattlesnake—coiled and ready to strike. And strike we do, shutting out the Maret Frogs on their home field, a bare dirt bowl surrounded by granite buildings in the heart of Washington, DC, 16-0. The victory is doubly sweet for Jerry because not only has he soundly beaten the Frogs, but their coach, Nick Kissoff, "the Mad Russian," Jerry's nemesis, is denied his opportunity for a league championship.

Jerry steps onto the bus ferrying us back to the Maret campus, pumps his fist like the drive wheel of a locomotive, and the chanting begins, "Goodson, Goodson, Goodson." Standing at the head of the aisle, one foot perched on top of a cooler, he beams as he rides the wave of exhilaration flowing from the team.

"All right, all right," he repeats still grinning from ear to ear as the chanting begins to subside, "It's not me … it's all twenty-five of you playing together as a team who deserve this victory. You should be chanting 'Eagles, Eagles, Eagles,' not my name. You did it, not me." With that a clatter of helmets against the roof of the bus goes up from the players along with an incipient "Eagles," which trails off as quickly as it begins when Jerry puts his two little fingers in his mouth and produces the high-pitched whistle he is known for.

"Okay, let's be gentle with the bus, guys. It's got to get us back to the Beach."

Another halfhearted cheer goes up from the team for either the bus or the Beach, I'm not sure which.

"There are people out there," Jerry begins now that he has the team's full attention, "who didn't think you could overcome all the crap of the past two weeks. But you did. There are people out there who didn't think you could stop the Frog's Power-I running game or contend with their two NBA-sized tight ends. But you did. And you can thank Kirk Deavers—all five-feet nine of him—for putting the hit on big #89 that took him out of the game permanently. That guy was about twice your size, wasn't he, Kirk?" The chant of "Deavers, Deavers, Deavers" starts up as the players bang him on his shoulder pads good-naturedly.

"You know there are even people out there—loyal Eagle fans—who didn't believe we could whip the Frogs and get into the championship game against Model next Saturday without a certain former member of this team." A smattering of boos goes up from some of the white players at this obvious reference to Flip. "I'm not going to mention his name. I think you know who I'm referring to. But we proved all them wrong today and we'll prove them wrong again next weekend when we kick Model's butt and bring that championship trophy back to the Beach where it belongs!" As he hits this high note, Jerry punctuates it by pumping his fist skyward and giving out a rebel yell. At this the team erupts all over again.

On Tuesday afternoon following the Maret game, Gomer Godfrey summons Jerry to his office. Evidently, unbeknownst to Jerry, the bus driver sitting not three feet from him during his post-game speech, waiting to drive them back to campus, was a Maret supporter who carried Jerry's comments back to Nick Kissoff. Kissoff's letter to Gomer calls for Jerry's immediate resignation. What Kissoff is particularly upset about are Jerry's remarks which seemed to commend Kirk

Deavers for deliberately injuring one of his players and, thereby, ensuring our victory over the Frogs. However, as he explains to the three of us before practice that afternoon, he only meant to characterize the incident as a lucky break that turned the tide in our favor. He never suggested that Kirk was deliberately trying to injure the Maret tight end, who was a head taller and fifty pounds heavier than Kirk. And that Kissoff ought to know that injuries are a part of the game. So, with the train rolling toward the season finale with Model now and a conference championship nearly at hand, even Gomer Godfrey realizes that's it is time to clear the tracks and full steam ahead. He lets Jerry off with letters of apology to Kissoff and the injured player—nothing more than a slap on the wrist.

The Tri-State Conference championship game is held at a neutral site in suburban Maryland, outside of DC, between the only two teams undefeated in conference play—Model School for the Deaf and us. I discover quickly that playing Model, as Jerry has warned us, is like fighting a three-headed monster—if the size and sheer number of players don't intimidate you; if the "boom, boom, boom" of the bass drum on the sidelines, communicating the snap count to the Model players through vibrations doesn't get you; there are always the strangled vocal expressions emanating from the Model players during warm-ups that make one wonder if there's really a human being beneath those helmets and pads.

In the first half, we try to take advantage of their hearing impairment by sending a receiver in motion prior to the snap, challenging their defensive backs to try to communicate with each other about it in a split second. But we end up playing too cute for our own good, resulting in a big fat goose egg on our side of the scoreboard. Fortunately, our defensive scheme to stop their power running game works the way it was designed, stifling the Model offense. Halftime finds us deadlocked, 0-0.

In the second half, Jerry's decision to return to the wide-open misdirection offense that got us here turns out to be the correct one. In the 4th quarter, Coleman Freeman hits Steve Wilkinson, our big tight end, in the corner of the end zone on a fade pattern giving us a seven-point advantage. Then, late in the game, Jon McKinstry waltzes into the end zone untouched on a running play we haven't shown all year to seal the deal, 14-0. We have done it! We are the Tri-State Conference champions.

After the hoopla and the high-fives at game's end, Jerry gathers the team around him in the end zone: "For all the hard work you've put in and all the unbelievable crap you've had to put up with this year, nobody deserves this championship more than you guys. I know." His voice begins to crack ... "I know I don't deserve it." He's visibly choking back the tears now.

"What are you crying for, Coach?" Wilkinson calls out. "We won the championship. You're supposed to be happy."

"I am happy." He wipes away the tears. "I've never been happier, Steve."

At this, two of the players hoist him onto their shoulders and carry him across the field to receive the Model coach's congratulations and the championship trophy. A week after the season ends, Jerry is named Tri-State Conference Coach of the Year despite Nick Kissoff's objections.

21

One Friday afternoon a couple of weeks after our season has ended, on a weekend when the only traveling Michelle and I are planning is a trip to Aux Fruits de Mer on Saturday night, the football staff plus Jonathan Pope meet at Jerry's house. Our intent is to wring the last ounce of fun out of the football season by driving over to King George County to watch the Foxes take on the Onancock HS Blue Devils from the Eastern Shore of Virginia in a semifinal playoff game. Despite a steady afternoon drizzle all of us are in high spirits, anticipating an evening of lively camaraderie, without the pressure of having to worry about the outcome of a game. What I have not anticipated, though, is that this one game will reveal to me a coaching style so antithetical to Jerry's that from this night forward it will draw me to safe harbor like a lighthouse guiding my ship through the fog.

"Where were you last weekend, Spinach Head? I drove by your house, but I didn't see your car. Did you and Miss *Lemonde* go off somewhere?" Jerry needles, investing the pronunciation of Michelle's last name with mock solemnity to get a laugh, which he does.

"As a matter of fact, we did go off … What's with 'Spinach Head'? I thought I was 'Spinach Man.'"

"Same difference," he says chuckling to himself at the propitious use of his own pet phrase.

"Jerry, how can it be the same and different at the same time?" Whitey ponders running his hand through his sweet potato hair.

"It just can, Knothead. We've been through this with you at least a dozen times and you still don't get it," Bear chimes in.

"Let me see if I can help clear the waters, fellas."

"That'd be like trying to cleanse the entire Potomac with a squeegee," Jonathan cracks.

"If it's so simple, then you explain it, Mr. Basketball," fumes Whitey.

"Settle down for God's sake," I command. "Now here's the deal, Whitey. It's a paradox, see. That means it sounds like it can't be true but it is ... Are you with me so far?"

"Yeah," Whitey mumbles popping a Rolaids in his mouth.

"Okay, here it is. You ready? It's the same person—me—whether you call me 'Spinach Head' or 'Spinach Man.' Right? (Whitey nods) But it's different because they're two different names. You see?"

"That's not it," interrupts Bear.

"Yes, it is," I insist.

"Yeah, I think I see, but how can the difference be the same? They're still two different names. They have different letters."

Jonathan and I begin to break down in waves of laughter at the pure absurdity of his logic. Then, Jerry cuts in, "You're right, Whitey. They both have different letters just like "Whitey" and "Bear" do. But both names refer to the same knuckleheaded assistants. Now do you get it?"

"I think I do now. You never explained it like that before, Jerry. Now I see what you mean."

"He's pulling your leg, Whitey," Jonathan tells him with a look of mock disgust as Bear roars with laughter.

We ride along for a mile or so, our mirth subsiding into silence, examining each solitary house we pass, looking for any signs of life in the deepening darkness. There are few—just the occasional car which, like a fish in an aquarium, brushes past us heading toward the Beach.

"Mike, do you mind if I ask you a personal question?" Jonathan suddenly asks. "Where do you and Michelle go when you go off?"

"No, I don't mind at all, Jon. It's not like we're Bonnie and Clyde," I say with half a smile. "This past weekend we went down to Virginia Beach."

"Is that where you usually go?"

"During the cold weather it is because the hotel we stay at has a heated indoor pool, and we both like to swim."

"What hotel is it?"

"The Queen Anne."

"Is it on the beach?"

"Yes, on the beachside of Atlantic Avenue. Are you familiar with Virginia Beach?"

"Mary and I went there on our honeymoon, but we haven't been back since then … is the Queen Anne expensive?"

"Hey, what is this—twenty questions?" Jerry interrupts. "If a man wants to have an affair with another teacher, they should be able to do it without a lot of questions being asked."

"Whoa!" Bear exclaims. "Now we're getting into the heavy shit."

"Have you told Virginia how you feel on this matter?"

"Hey, I'm just tryin' to help you out. What's your business should stay your business, especially at the Beach, where if you fart loud enough, they'll be talkin' about it at Olive's at lunchtime."

"I know, Coach, and I appreciate it. I'm just teasing you."

"The only reason I'm asking for is what if Mary and I want to get away for a weekend? We'd like to stay someplace nice," Jonathan pleads chaffing his left wrist with his right hand, a nervous gesture I've seen him produce unconsciously before the tip-off of every basketball game he coaches.

"Don't worry about it, son. You won't be going anywhere until basketball season is over."

"You're right about that, Coach."

"Getting back to your question, Jon. The Queen Anne is a bit pricey, but on two teachers' salaries it's affordable … it'll probably run you fifty to sixty bucks a night … out-of-season."

King George has one of the most unusual high school stadiums I have ever visited. Unlike most, it is set down well below road level so that tonight—game night—the only thing I see as we approach it on Rte. 3 is a bowl of light spilling out into the darkness above it. By the time we find a place to park, the first half has already begun. Onancock is leading, 7-0. We make our way through the steady drizzle to the Blue Devil's side of the field where there are empty seats high up in the stands from which we can get a bird's eye view of the action on the field. The Blue Devils, a team seemingly composed entirely of black players, runs the Wishbone, an effective ball-control offense that is less than exhilarating to watch unless you're an Onancock fan—option right, option left, reverse option, speed option, off-tackle lead, but nary a single pass. If you've seen one wishbone team, you've seen them all. Unfortunately, for King George no matter how many times they see it, they can't seem to stop it, as Onancock advances steadily downfield almost every time they have the ball—three or four or five yards at a pop. Soon they have built a 21-0 lead, and with the Foxes' own inability to generate any offense, the Blue Devils seem to have the game well in hand by halftime.

In the second half, Jerry directs my attention to the Onancock sideline. Once there, I can hardly take my eyes off of what I can only characterize as the most unique sideline situation I've ever witnessed in my coaching career, then or since. First of all, when it is time to punt or receive a punt or time to switch from offense to defense or vice versa, there is no coach yelling and gesticulating in an effort to assemble the proper players to send on the field. In fact, there don't appear to be any assistant coaches at all along the Blue Devils' sideline though they must be there somewhere. I scan the Onancock sideline between plays, but I can't seem to locate them. Assistant coaches or no assistant coaches, the players who will be needed in the game shortly huddle calmly on the sideline, account for their teammates, and then take the field like clock-work. I quickly realize that this manner of coaching is diametrically opposed to Jerry's style of communicating at full throttle with incandescent intensity.

I am also intrigued by the fact that Onancock doesn't shuttle players carrying plays into the offensive huddle between downs. I do notice Onancock's black quarterback—#11—conferring with a tall, gray-haired man in a dark green rain slicker between each offensive series, but based on what I see taking place on the field, my conclusion is that #11 is the one making all the play calls. Quite a responsibility, particularly in a playoff game, I think to myself. When I point this out to Jerry, he just shrugs and remarks that they might be hand signaling the plays in. So, I watch intently for this among the players or from the gray-haired man along the sideline, but I'm unable to detect it.

The longer I watch the easier it becomes to believe in the notion that the Onancock players are controlling the game—they are calling the offensive plays, they are making the defensive calls, they are doing the substituting, they are correcting their teammates when they make an error, they are making the necessary adjustments—they are in charge. They have not just been taught how to block and tackle and catch and throw, they have been taught how to run the whole show. But despite what my eyes tell me, I still refuse to believe that there isn't someone on the Onancock sideline who's at the helm of their ship. So, I turn my attention back to the tall, gray-haired man in the rain slicker. He seems to be the only person resembling an authority figure on the Blue Devils' side of the field.

For most of the game, he occupies a space just to the left of their bench, three or four yards off the sideline, where he can see most of the playing field. He only alters his location to assure himself of a fuller view of the action on the field. He doesn't pace the sideline in front of the players, shouting criticism or encouragement to those on the playing field. Nor does he revile the referees or edge out onto the field to question a call. He talks with players who approach him, particularly #11, or those whose attention he summons with an unobtrusive wave of his hand. There is no arm waving, facemask grabbing, or chin-to-chin communication in his relationship with his players. He makes no outward show of disgust when one of his players makes a mistake or joy when they do something well. However, he does allow himself a singular expression of emotion whenever the Blue Devils score; elbows bent, he raises both hands to shoulder level while clenching his fists. That is all. It is as if he has done all his coaching, prepared his team for every eventuality, and taught all his lessons during the week prior to the game, and now he is content to stand back and enjoy the fruits of his labor, while making an occasional coaching point. I watch silently, consumed by this vision.

22

One overcast Sunday afternoon in the heart of January, Michelle and I are driving back to the Beach after spending the weekend with my parents in Northern Virginia. The weatherman has been calling for a heavy accumulation of snow all day long, but we do not see the first flakes until we begin heading south on I-95. By the time we reach Fredericksburg, we can barely see the lines on the road five feet in front of us, and the traffic has slowed to a crawl. On the radio the weatherman is calling for twelve to eighteen inches by morning. We count this a blessing. If there is that much snow on the ground by tomorrow morning, we will not have school for a week at the Beach.

We take the Falmouth exit off I-95—finally free of its congestion—and jog over to Route 3. Once we are on it the snow seems to thicken, if that is possible; all we can do is creep along in the waning light at twenty-five miles per hour in the Blue Bunny, thanking the German automotive gods for mounting the engine in the rear. Thankfully, there is very little traffic on 3. But just before it narrows from four lanes to two, through the skein of swirling snowflakes, Michelle spies a white compact car which has slid off the road and is quickly blending in with drift it rests in. Then we spot a black man in a familiar red and blue Eagles jacket standing on the shoulder of the road waving his arms over his head.

"Stop!" Michelle commands. "It's Rondell."

I gently pump the brakes but still nearly end up in the same ditch with Rondell's car. When he opens the backdoor of the Bunny and sticks his head inside, I say, "Hey, stranger, do you want a lift or are planning on walking back to the Beach?"

"Let me in. I'm sure glad you two came along when you did, or I might end up as one frozen Tootsie Roll." We all laugh heartily.

"Rondell, what are you doing out in this terrible weather?" Michelle asks.

"I'd gone up to the Mall to look for some tunes. But I must have lost track of time because when I came outside, it had started snowing pretty heavily. I thought I could make it back to the Beach, but those old bald tires of mine had me spinnin' my wheels and slidin' all over the road until I ended up in that ditch back there where the road bends to the left."

"How long had you been there?"

"No more than five or ten minutes."

"You are lucky because we haven't seen a single car along this stretch of 3 since we got on it. You might have frozen to death in this blizzard before anybody had come along and found you … Where's you heavy coat, man? That Eagles jacket is not going to keep you warm in this storm."

"I know. I know. Hey, but the company is good, you know," he says with a broad smile. "What are y'all doing out on a night like this?"

"We had just left Michael's parents' house," Michelle explains, "when we saw the first flakes. It didn't look too bad then, but the snow came down so fast that by the time we got to Fredericksburg we could hardly see the road in front of us."

"Mike, do you have snow tires? Can we make it to the Beach?"

"I hope so. If we can make it to the Bluff, we can stop at my house and ride out this blizzard. I don't think we'll have to worry about school tomorrow, do you?"

They both nod in agreement.

As we crawl along, the asphalt and the lane lines disappear beneath a layer of white. All I can do is keep the tires rolling in the fast-disappearing ruts worn by previous vehicles. I know if I can just keep the car moving forward, we have a good chance of reaching the Bluff. Finally, the road sinks down to just above water level as we reach Potomac Beach, passing the shrouded forms of Williamson's and the Dancing Crab on our left. Then, up the hill to Locust, take a left, feel our way to the end of the road, take a left onto Mimosa, and we've made it.

"Good driving, Sugar."

"Yeah, way to go, Coach," Rondell says clapping me on the back. "I didn't think we were going to make it, but you got us here. Good job, Brother!"

"Big bubbles, no troubles! Was there ever any doubt?"

There are at least six inches of snow on the kitchen steps as we climb them gingerly, clinging to the handrail. Yet, the storm shows no sign of abating, and with night approaching it is getting darker and colder by the minute. As I fiddle with my keys, I throw out the thought that this would be a great time to walk out on the Bluff and watch the snow falling on the river. But this idea is quickly nixed by Michelle, who's afraid of accidentally stepping off the edge of the Bluff in the swirling snow and Rondell, who's just plain freezing in his Eagles jacket. So, we retire to the warmth of my little two-bedroom house, sip a little wine, and then head off to bed with the wind off the river singing its siren song

When I awake, the storm has passed, but it has left behind its signature—snowdrifts obscuring the bottom half of the Blue Bunny and extending upward to the sill of the living room window. The snow is closer to twenty-four inches than twelve, making the roads impassable until they are plowed. We are in for a bout of communal living, it seems. I've socialized with Rondell on several occasions since the dinner cruise, but this will give us a chance to get to know each other a lot better. I call Michelle to come and see, knowing that Rondell will hear me and get up also.

"Now, this is what I call a real snowstorm. Sweetheart, have you ever seen this much snow at the Beach before?"

"Never. I've never seen this much snow anywhere ... ever."

"Rondell, come check out this snow. It looks like you're going to be stuck here a while, Bro, unless you're up for walking home."

"No way!"

More than once during our four-day hibernation together, the conversation turns to Jerry Goodson and Columbia Beach football, but Rondell seems to studiously avoid bringing up the Flip Richmond incident and my promise to Jerry makes me hesitant to discuss it. Three nights into our snowy sojourn, however, while sitting around the tube getting bored, Rondell breaks the ice on this sore subject. "Mike, do you mind if I ask you about something? And you don't have to talk about it if you don't want to. Just let me know and I'll drop the subject," he says scratching two days worth of beard on his chin.

"Depends on what you want to talk about. If it's about Michelle and me, we can't go there," I answer with mock gravity.

"No, you know I wouldn't ask you about that."

"Michael," Michelle intones scolding me. "Rondell, he's just putting you on. He knows you wouldn't ask about that."

"Yeah, I know," he says, his mouth twisted into crooked smile. "What I want to ask you about is the night Flip went off on the sideline and stripped off his uniform during the game. Who were you playing? Trinity Episcopal?"

"Yeah."

"You know I wasn't there that night. I was tending bar at a wedding party over at Dahlgren. So, I missed all the excitement."

"What do you want to know?"

"What happened? I mean I've heard stories, but you were right there in the middle of it, weren't you?"

"Yes, I guess I was in the middle of it since I was the one who got punched," I say with enough sarcasm in my voice to dry paint.

"Yeah, but how did you end up takin' the punch. I heard Flip was actually swingin' at Jerry. Jerry must have said something that made him go off."

"Well, actually, Jerry asked me not to tell anyone what he'd said to Flip that set him off that night … But if you promise that what I'm going to say to you will never leave this room, I'll tell you. And Michelle doesn't even know this, so this is some high-level shit I'm talking about here. If it got out—and you know how fast shit travels at the Beach—Jerry would not be at all happy with me because I'm sure he thinks that, besides Flip, he and I were the only ones who heard what he said that night."

"Come on, man, you know me better than that. Who am I gonna tell? I heard Jerry told Godfrey that all he said to Flip was that he didn't have his head screwed on right."

"Yeah, I've heard that too. But does that sound to you like something that would cause a player to try to punch out a coach, not to mention quitting on the team in the middle of a game?"

"Not really … You know what he really said though don't you; you were right there."

"All right, what he said was, 'Forget Flip! He's got his head up his ass.'"

"That's all he said? He didn't curse him? That doesn't seem like enough to set someone off the way Flip went off."

"Well, in this case, coming in the middle of the game, with Flip's ankle giving him fits, it was sufficient, believe me."

"Oh, I believe you, no doubt, brother."

"But the worst part of the situation was Jerry embarrassing him in front of the team. That's what totally set him off. Of course, that's the one thing Jerry had cautioned us against doing when he told us back in September that Flip would be rejoining the team, 'Don't cut him any slack, but don't embarrass him in front of the team either.' Then, he goes ahead and contradicts himself ... but I'm sure he didn't do it on purpose; he just lost his temper for a moment in the heat of the game, that's all."

"Just like Flip did," Michelle repeats as though talking to herself, "just like Flip."

"Yeah, right. He's not supposed to lose his temper. He's the head coach. When he went ballistic, that opened the door for Flip to go off, don't you see."

"You're probably right, Rondell. But it's over now, man. It's history. Forget it."

"I won't have any problem forgetting it; it's not my history. You're the one who has to worry about forgetting it."

"What do you mean?"

"It's your history. You were part of the staff it happened to. It's not just Jerry, although he's the main one. It's a reflection on the whole coaching staff ... on the whole school for that matter. What you have to decide, Mike, is whether you want to be associated with that style of coaching. Or, do you have your own style—a different style? You know every successful coach has got to have his own identity—his own way of doing things—his own set of beliefs. You want to be a head coach one day, don't you?"

"Yes."

"Well, are you going to coach like Jerry Goodson or are you going to coach like Michael Burns? Do you see my point?"

"He's got a point, Sugar."

"Yes, I agree Rondell has a point," I say sipping my wine, "but it's too late."

"Too late for what, man?"

"I've already seen the light."

"What … that Onancock thing you told me about?"

"Yes, that Onancock thing."

"Come on, Mike. I talked to Jerry about that, and he said there had to have been assistant coaches there on the sidelines organizing things. You must have just overlooked them. How could the players have been so well prepared in the first place if there was only one coach running the show during the week? Tell me that."

"I know what I saw, Rondell. Did Jerry say he saw assistant coaches? … No, I don't think so."

"What's so important about the assistant coaches anyway?" Michelle chimes in. "I thought it was the demeanor of the one coach you did see that impressed you, Sugar."

"That's right! Rondell, what was most impressive about this guy's coaching style was the way he talked to his players, how he commanded their attention, his self-control … his presence. If I could emulate those qualities, I'd be a great coach," I say taking Michelle's hand in mine.

"I think so too, but how are you going to be that kind of coach on this staff? Jerry's the exact opposite of that."

"Rondell, what it sounds like you're saying is that in order to find myself I'll have to say good-bye to the Beach. I don't see how I can do that; I just got here. And besides, I couldn't leave Michelle behind. She's everything to me now."

"I understand completely, my man. You might have to put the future on hold while you take from your experience here whatever it's worth. There's no reason you can't stay here and continue to learn from Jerry; he's got a lot to offer—both positively and negatively—if you get my meaning. So, when things start to get crazy next year—as they surely will with Jerry at the helm—just remember this little conversation and keep your wits about you. All you have to do to survive here is to save your soul while everybody else is losing his."

On Wednesday evening they finally plow Mimosa. Thursday morning the three of us dig my car out of the drifts in the driveway so I can take Rondell home. In spite of the good times we've shared over the past few days, he is anxious to change out of the clothes he's been wearing since Sunday. When I pull up in front of his cottage on Washington Street, we spend a few minutes talking about the snow and school and our good luck in coming along to rescue him when we did. The only thing that goes unspoken is how what has passed between us these past four days has turned familiarity into friendship.

23

One morning in the middle of April I raise my head from the pillow and find spring has spread its sunshine and warmth across the Earth, beckoning merry birds to the blue sky, inciting insects to industry, and calling forth colors where there previously have been none. But among springtime's vernal bounty—the crocus, the jonquils, the tulips, the mock orange, and the azaleas—also thrive the bull whistle, ironweed, ragweed and dandelion. So, it is among my human relations this spring—some are blossoms while others are weeds.

As my relationship with Michelle blooms in a hundred unexpected shades, Lucy Free's endless plying and prattling and importuning seem to increase in direct proportion to each passing day in the Media Center. Hers is a unique form of hospitality. During first semester, she inaugurated the "massage/conversation" communication technique. This usually took place in the morning when the library was empty except for the occasional library aide. I might have been sitting or standing at the checkout desk, surveying the stacks or thumbing through the overdues with my back to Lucy's office. First, I would have detected the wooden clack of her approaching high heels; then, I would have felt her hand running up and down my back as she commented on some mundane issue—a bit of school gossip that is making the rounds, whose progress has been fueled by Lucy, or some local news item she has an opinion on, or what duty "that little nigger, Alvin" (one of her aides) has failed to carry out the previous day, or what the weather is going to be like that day. It hardly matters what we talk about as long as she continues the back massage to the point of annoyance, on my part, and to the point of attention gained, on hers.

In the spring, however, she comes up with a variation on the "massage/conversation" technique, which I term the "shoulder-to-shoulder, hip-to-hip connection." Once again the Media Center might be empty or nearly so, and I would be leaning on the checkout desk, staring out into space. I might be daydreaming on what I have to do after school that day, or where we will eat dinner that night, or how slowly the clock on the wall seems to be running, or Michelle in all her naked glory when I might feel someone lodged against my side, hip-to-hip, shoulder-to-shoulder, like a piece of food that can't be expelled from between my teeth no matter what method of extrication I employ. The subject of her conversation does not differ markedly from that broached during the "massage/conversation" stage of our relationship, but with this new technique Lucy enjoys two points of physical contact rather than just one while she titter tatters. I, on the other hand, can only stare straight ahead, responding as briefly as possible to her queries, in the hope of discouraging any further conversation.

At times, I feel like I am some sort of harlequin of human relations, reconciling within myself black and white, darkness and light. Day by day, my working relationship with Lucy Free becomes more tiresome and tedious, yet with each passing week my romance with Michelle grows bolder and more adventuresome. One Saturday morning in mid April, a day filled with sunlight and possibility beneath a seamless blue sky, I pack Michelle's marinated chicken wings, her savory potato salad, and carrot and celery sticks—my contribution to the victuals—along with a bottle of dry (very dry) Chardonnay in the back of the Blue Bunny, and we head out on Route 3 towards the Blue Ridge Mountains west of Culpeper.

Just past Lignum, without a car in sight, the sunlight pouring through the windshield takes control, spreading over us like a blanket, leaving us relaxed and aroused. Michelle leans over and encircles my neck with her arms. She pulls herself close to me and kisses my neck behind my ear, sending a shiver through me. Facing forward, I hold the car steady while she slowly works her mouth over my ear and circles the inside of it with her tongue, her breath filling my ear with warmth. With my eyes locked on the road, I grasp her naked thigh in my hand, squeezing it in rhythm with every wave of passion that surges through me. Suddenly, she places her hand over mine and guides it to her sex, rising rhythmically against my stroking fingers, kissing my ear and moaning. I find the opening in the crotch of her shorts, slide the strip of her panties aside, and thrust my finger deep inside her vagina, finding it as wet as a water lily. She gasps as I plunge inside her again and again until she can stand no more. Then, she comes, crossing her long thighs over my hand driving my finger deeper inside her while, at the same time, attaching herself to my neck like a suckling. It's all I can do to keep my eyes open and the car on the road as we revel in a pleasure so titillating and intense that I barely notice as Rte. 3 turns into 29 South and the traffic picks up.

"Oh, Michael, you make me feel so good," she whispers in my ear.

"I'm glad … so glad. You want to stop at a motel and get a room?"

"Do you know of a cheap one around here? Where are we? Near Culpeper?" she asks straightening her shorts.

"Just outside of it. I'm not sure what they have here. I think there's a Holiday Inn out here on the bypass, but I don't know if we've passed it or not."

"Oh, that'll be too expensive. But just hold onto that thought till we get back to the Beach," she says with smile.

She knows I will.

Instead of getting off 29 at Culpeper, we continue south towards Charlottesville, still enjoying the afterglow of our erotic play. Then, we turn at Madison and parallel a branch of the Rapidan River through Banco, Criglersville, and Syria up into the foothills of the Blue Ridge. By the time the gravel road we've been traveling on turns to dirt, the Rapidan has narrowed to no more than a stream strewn with granite boulders of varying size. I pull off onto the side of the road. We check behind us to see if there are any following vehicles; then, we strip down to our swimsuits and tennis shoes. Our plan is to hike the Rapidan upstream to a cool mountain pool to soak in, driving away the midday heat. Since there is no path beside the stream, we find the best way to negotiate it is to wade through the water, snaking around the larger boulders so that we won't have to scramble over them in our suits. After fifteen minutes of hiking, the stream narrows to a creek with few if any pools large enough to immerse our bodies in. Just a few yards above us, though, is a moss-covered boulder with a rounded flat side like a slanted table top, shining in the sunlight coming through the pines. Upon reaching it, we lie back on its warm, grainy surface, turning our faces into the sun as we slowly catch our breath.

"I guess I made a mistake; we should have gone downstream," Michelle says pulling her feet up and resting her chin on her knees in the best impression of a pout I've seen her put on since I met her.

"I wouldn't call this morning's activity on the way here 'a mistake,'" I say trying to tease her out of her disappointment.

"Oh no, I didn't mean that … *that* was wonderful. I told you that, silly." She leans back on the rock and closes her eyes, a smile on her face. "I just meant if we want to swim, we'd better …"

"Shhhhh," I whisper putting my forefinger to her lips. "Keep your eyes closed and just listen for a minute … what do you hear?"

"Nothing … nothing but birds and insects."

"Keep your eyes closed and see if you can hear anybody else out here except us," I say as I begin gently tracing an imaginary line with my index finger along the top of her swimsuit bottom, then working my way along her crotch line to her sex. She shudders.

"Michael, what are you doing?" she asks without opening her eyes.

"Just listen. There's nobody out here but us," I say slowly inching her swimsuit bottom down while nuzzling her neck.

"Michael, do you think we should?"

"Yes."

She's still wet as rain. When I enter her, she moans in surrender. We make love on our own rock in the open air as if we are the only two people left alive on the planet.

24

"I've been giving some thought lately to what Rondell had to say," I tell Michelle as we approach the intersection of Rte. 301 (The Blue Star Memorial Highway) and 205. Against her best advice, I cross over 301 and continue west toward Fredericksburg where we'll connect with I-95 on a sticky Friday afternoon in May. She had lobbied for a left onto 301 and another left onto Rte. 17 south at Port Royal, which would lead us along the Rappahannock River to Tidewater and eventually Nags Head on the North Carolina coast. With the Outer Banks lying a good six hours south of the Beach, I have opted instead for the fastest (I hope or I'll never hear the end of it) and the most direct route south, with arrival some time between nine and ten that evening. But I-95 is our enemy this afternoon, not our friend. Just below Ladysmith the southbound traffic slows to a crawl, giving us the opportunity to turn our conversation back to its original subject—Rondell's advice.

"I don't remember everything Rondell said that night, but the one thing I do recall was him talking about the need for you to create your own coaching identity. Is that what you're referring to?"

"That and the part about saving my soul when everyone else is losing theirs. That struck me then and it still strikes a chord in me now ... what are you so grouchy about?"

"I don't know ... the traffic I guess." Michelle responds, curling and uncurling strands of blonde hair around her forefinger.

"There must have been an accident," I say stretching myself out of the driver's side window in futility. "Anyway ... the way I see it, these two things are connected ... I can't hope to save my soul if I don't know what's important to me … what I value … can I? When it comes down to crunch time next year or down the road somewhere, who am I going to be … Jerry Goodson or Michael Burns?" I pause and watch Michelle's face to see what emotions are playing across it. All I find is myself reflected in the hardness of her unsmiling eyes. The traffic has now stopped altogether.

"Go ahead; I'm listening," she says evenly.

"It's not like I don't know what I want. I know what kind of football coach I want to be. I've seen it. And, as much as I like Jerry and as much as he's done for me, it's not him I want to model myself after. But I know I could very easily end up like him. Now and then, I catch myself ranting and raving at practice and on the sidelines, and I wonder where all this emotion is coming from and I realize I'm mimicking Jerry. I'm acting just like him. And do you want to know why, Michelle? Do you?"

"Yes, tell me, Michael."

"Because it's acceptable, that's why. The message has been passed down that it's okay to act this way. That's all."

"If it's such a big problem for you, silly, let it go. Just don't do it. Just be yourself and don't worry about Jerry."

"It's not that simple."

All of a sudden, I realize the traffic ahead of us is beginning to unlimber. I turn my attention back to driving and leave my last comment floating between us in midair. I check the time. It's almost 5:30 and we haven't even reached Richmond yet. It's going to be a late arrival I tell myself. The traffic on I-95 thins out below Petersburg, and we make up lost time as the evening sun burns a hole in the sky off to our right. We ride silently, listening to our own thoughts and occasionally searching the radio dial for traveling music to fill the space between us until we reach the Weldon exit just below the North Carolina line. There, we turn off onto 301 south as we start skittering across the eastern part of the state like a beach crab through one little tobacco town after another—Scotland Neck, Hobgood, Oak City, Hamilton, Williamston, Plymouth, and Columbia—to the Outer Banks. It's a little after 7:30 p.m.with the sun slipping down behind us. It'll be dark by the time we reach the coast.

"It's not like coaching is just bite your tongue and hope for the best. Coaching, especially coaching football, is all about controlling players—controlling your team, as much as any one person can," I start out again.

"What do you mean?" Michelle asks turning toward me with a quizzical look on her face as though what I've just said has come to her out of the clear blue.

"When I say it's not that simple, I mean some coaches try to control their team by building a bridge of trust between themselves and their players, others resort to fear to try to establish control. But both types of coaches realize subconsciously that the coach who can control his players more effectively is the coach who has the best chance of being successful."

"Go on. We know what category Jerry falls into. But, Michael, you're not that way, are you?"

"Oh, I have to admit with all the success we were having last year, I bought into Jerry's system. But it left a bad taste in my mouth, especially after the incident with Flip. And then seeing that coach from Onancock's coaching style convinced me there must be a better way. But some coaches, Jerry included, seem to believe that if they allow the kids to get too close to them, they'll lose the players' respect. So, they keep them at arms length—yelling and screaming and intimidating. I don't want to be that kind of coach, Michelle."

"Don't worry, Sugar," she says reaching over and massaging the back of my neck. "You're not going to be."

"But I could. That's the problem. Don't you see that if I stay at the Beach, either I'll conform to Jerry's style just like I did this past season, or I'll make a conscious effort to be different and end up being ostracized. And when that happens, I'll be moving on anyway. So, I might as well begin looking for a coaching situation that offers me an outlook I can relate to while the iron is still hot and Jerry will give me a good recommendation. Besides, I'm not looking forward to spending another year in the library with you-know-who. I'm just a little sick and tired, Michelle, of her putting her hands all over me everyday."

"Lucy? She's harmless, Michael. You know that. She was brought up here in the South; that's just her way of being friendly. If it bothers you that much, just ask her in a nice way to refrain and I'm sure she will."

"I shouldn't have to ask her," I explode. "It's not professional. She should know that without me having to tell her. And it's not just the sexual harassment … it's her obvious racial prejudice, too. There's no place in public education for a person like her. The school administration needs to know about her. She needs to be put out to pasture. That's for damn sure!"

"Cool down, Sugar! Do you want me to talk to her? I think she'll listen to me … Give me a chance to speak to her before you go off half-cocked and do something you'll regret."

"That's not what I'm after."

"Well, what is it you do want, Michael Burns?" Michelle says turning halfway around in her seat so she's facing me with her back against the passenger-side door. "Nothing seems to please you. You win a championship in football—the first championship the Beach has won in years—and you're not happy. You can't wait to leave. Not only that but you have the cushiest position in the school—working in the Media Center—a position other teachers would kill for and you're dissatisfied. What is it that you do want besides getting Lucy fired?" Her eyes are flashing like lightning over the Potomac now. I've never seen her this upset.

"All I want is for us to be together," I say in the calmest voice I can summon, trying to mitigate her fury. "I want you to say you'll come with me if I do decide to leave. That's all. That's more important than anything else in the world right now."

"Listen, Sugar, I love you in the worst sort of way, but I don't know if I can commit myself to running around from school to school while you look for the perfect coaching position, not knowing from year to year where we'll be or if I'll have a job. I have to work too, you know. I can't just sit home watching the Soaps. I've got to have something that fulfills me."

"Don't worry. I'll make sure you have a job, too. I promise we won't go anyplace where we both don't have jobs," I say with a dismissive wave of my hand. "Don't worry about that now."

"I do worry about it. I worry about it a lot, particularly after all you've said tonight."

I reach over and gently rub her thigh until I coax her into putting her hand on top of mine. We sail on into the darkness through little towns lit up by single convenience stores and surrounded by inky swampland. Casting our light ahead of us into the murkiness of the night, we are transfixed by the broken white lines on Route 64 and lost in our own thoughts. All of a sudden, just a mile or two east of Creswell, a shadow crosses our windshield from right to left so swiftly that I barely have time to reach for the brake. At first I mistake it for a deer, but the upturned metal on its receding hooves tells a different story. It's a rider-less horse galloping blindly through the night.

"Oh, my God, Michael, what was that?" Michelle cries.

"I think it was a horse … do you realize that if we'd been going just a tad faster, we'd have reached that spot in the road one or two seconds sooner, and there'd be three dead bodies back there on the road now?"

"Oh, God, don't say that … don't even think that. I don't want to go that way," she says between deep breaths.

"We got lucky there, Sweetheart … really lucky. I never even saw that damn horse until it was right in front of me."

She takes my hand and places it over her left breast, "Feel my heart; it's pounding."

"I can feel it, but are you sure it's not just my hand on your breast that's doing it?" I say with the dry chuckle of a man who's just escaped the gallows.

When we finally reach Manteo, the night sky illuminated by ground lights shines like an ebony stone. We cross Croatan Sound and head north on 158 to Nags Head, passing the largest sand dunes in the U.S. staked down off to our left like sleeping elephants. Farther along we are dazzled by a Victorian bed and breakfast lit up like an ocean liner, floating among the rolling dunes around Kitty Hawk, where the Wright Brothers conquered gravity for a moment in 1903. But we don't stop there. I ignore 158 as it turns back northwest across Albemarle Sound, and I continue straight up north on a skinny stretch of road until we reach an old haunting ground of mine from my undergraduate days at East Carolina University—Duck. It is just as I remember it—nothing but sand dunes and a few scattered beach houses set back off Rte. 12 away from the ocean. I slow down and creep along on the asphalt surface of the road as it eventually leads us through the gaping gate of a sagging chain link fence, finally petering out, turning into hard-packed sand. This is the signal that we have reached the old artillery range. I pull the Bunny onto the shoulder and park keeping the wheels firmly planted on solid ground away from the loose sand that lines the road, knowing if we slip into any of the loose stuff, there'll be the devil to pay to get us out.

By the light of my flashlight, we drag beach blankets and a cooler of chilled Chardonnay over the dunes toward the roar of the ocean. As we trudge along, I remind Michelle to keep an eye out for any live shells left over from WWII. At this, she scurries up close behind me, holding onto the waistband of my shorts, as I play point man forging a safe path across the sand. Duck had been used during WWII as an artillery range by Allied battlewagons cruising off the coast of North Carolina. Except for a few adventurous individuals seeking solitude on this narrow finger of sand, it remains nearly as deserted today as it was during the war. Although I catch an occasional glint of something metallic in my beam, the chances of encountering a live shell on our trek are probably more than I know—but less than I suspect.

Reaching the crest of a notch line between two humps of sand, we find the sea below us, its glistening back rolling like a primeval beast beneath the full moon. We race down the side of the dune to the beach with our blankets flung out behind us like gypsy flags. Crossing the flat, moist surface of the sand, we are drawn to the water's edge by the waves whispering to themselves at low tide. Freeing ourselves of our possessions, we immediately set about gathering driftwood to kindle a fire and drink our wine fearlessly beside the ocean. There is nobody here but us. As the fire slowly dies, our passion rises; so we make love with the stars smiling down, wringing the last ounce of energy out of ourselves after a long day. Then, fading fast, we wrap ourselves in our beach blankets and succumb to sleep face down on the beach. When we finally are able to rouse ourselves the next morning, we find that the brilliant sun has been up long before us and has done its work. We quickly discover that our backs and the backs of our legs—especially Michelle's, who has on nothing but panties and a bra—have taken on a scarlet hue quite painful to the touch.

25

A few days after our return from Duck, days spent with Michelle administering final exams in French and me rescuing library books and audio/visual equipment from reasons why they shouldn't be returned, I find a note in my box from Mr. Godfrey instructing me in a tone at once both matter-of-fact and ominous that Dr. Roberson would like to meet with me at my earliest convenience regarding a matter of some urgency. The fact that Gomer has served as go-between indicates to me that he knows what the nature of the summons is, just as I do. There are few secrets in education (only the last person to hear them) because there are too many tongues to tell them and too many ears to hear them. So, it's no secret that I am not happy with the situation in the library. It's no secret that Lucy's endless river of gossip, her smoke-rasped voice, and her hands working overtime have all rubbed me the wrong way—literally and figuratively. The bow of my frustration was notched and strung early in the school year. With each passing day's indignities, I have drawn back the bowstring, quarter inch by quarter inch, until I'm ready now to let fly my arrow of protest, hoping it will find its mark. The notes I have taken over the course of the school year—at Jerry's suggestion—concerning Lucy's sexual harassment and racial prejudice, I have assembled in a letter directed to Mr. Roberson's attention.

Why, after a successful football season, do I chose to court disaster instead of letting things run their course? Why do I choose to make an issue of Lucy's lechery, something that has been going on for years before I ever arrived and will probably continue after I'm gone? And

why am I willing to put my career at risk over some prune-faced fol-
lower of Melville Dewey when I've never said a word to anyone about
Jerry's little sideline run-in with Flip Richmond, except Rondell and
Michelle? As I've reminded Michelle more than once, I don't believe
there is a place in education for someone like Lucy Free. But deep down
what I feel for Lucy is something closer to disgust than disenchantment.

Some superintendents are known for their genuine compassion for
students, some for their forward-looking philosophy of education, and
still others for their concern for the needs of their teachers. Dr. L. Ran-
dall Roberson, A.K.A. "Robo," is, on the other hand, known for his
mane of silver hair, which when carefully parted on the left and combed
back, forms a wave breaking on the beach just above his right ear and
for his silver tongue, which is kept well-oiled and lubricated for any for-
mal occasion that might arise in the course of any given school day.

When I enter his office, he is busy doing some housekeeping, dusting
stray cigarette ashes from his desktop with a miniature hot pink duster
(a gift, no doubt, from one of this adoring secretaries). As the signs say,
"Our Campus Is Smoke-free," except for Robo's office that is. He lights
another cigarette.

"Coach Burns, glad you could make it. Have a seat," he says giving
my outstretched hand the quick squeeze and release and then indicating
with an open palm the two chairs in front of his desk. "How do you
like Columbia Beach?" he asks as though Gomer Godfrey had just
given me the first time once over of the school and the town.

Whenever Robo opens his mouth to speak, I can't take my eyes off
the inside of his lower lip. He appears to have a canker the size of a
miniature pencil eraser hanging off it. *"Benign or malignant?" I wonder
silently unable to tear my eyes away from it.*

"Fine, sir. I like it fine … it's one of the most unique places I've ever worked, Dr. Roberson."

"Then, aside from this little misunderstanding with Ms. Free, you've enjoyed your time hear at the Beach?" But before I can respond to his question, he adds. "I understand you've made some strong relationships here this year. Coach Goodson speaks very highly of you and Ms. Lemonde …"

"Yes, sir." Uncomfortable with the direction the conversation seems to be heading, I interrupt him off. "The whole faculty has gone out of its way to make me feel welcome … and I really appreciate that, not being from around here."

"Even Ms. Free?"

"No, well, I don't think I'd be sitting here talking with you today if everything were fine in the library."

"How long has this situation with Ms. Free been going on, Mr. Burns?" His use of "Mister" instead of "Coach" does not go unnoticed. I uncross and recross my legs and sit up a little straighter in my chair.

"As I indicated in the communication I sent you, the incident with the lamp took place in the library on the first day I met her."

"Oh, yes, she rubbed against you with her leg. Wasn't that it?"

"Yes."

"Are you sure this was deliberate on her part? Could it have just been an accident?"

"I might be able to buy that, Dr. Roberson, if it weren't for the pattern of physical contact that continued throughout the rest of the school year. Why, even that same day as I was leaving the library, she grabbed my hand in both of hers and placed it between her breasts. Maybe that's just her way of shaking hands, I don't know. Maybe she does that with everyone. But I felt a little uncomfortable, to say the least.

"Right. Coach, I'm sure you believe you're telling the truth, but I've known Lucy ever since I accepted the superintendent position here at the Beach twelve years ago, and I've never received a complaint of this nature about her before by either another faculty member, a member of the community, or even—Lord forbid—a student." He lights another cigarette. "Do you mind if I smoke?" he asks.

"No, that's fine." As if anything I could say would keep him from smoking.

"Coach, you not being from around here puts me in mind that you may not be aware that Lucy—excuse my familiarity—Ms. Free is a native of the Northern Neck. From what I understand, she was born and raised in King George County. Her parents had a farm down toward the Potomac on the other side of 301. Lived here all her life. And the people 'round here, if they like someone, they are not afraid to show it … you know, 'hands on,' so to speak. Now, I've had a chance to talk to Ms. Free a little bit about this, and I'm going to speak to her again after we talk, but she tells me she hasn't treated you any differently than any other male teacher at the high school. And like I said, we've never had any complaints of this nature regarding her behavior prior to this one of yours. Of course, being in the Media Center all day with her, I can see how there'd be more opportunity for 'friendly' physical contact … Of course, there's also more opportunity to get on each other's nerves being cooped up like a couple of chickens in that library eight hours a day."

He pauses a moment allowing me to respond, but I can see what I'm up against. I just lick my lips and stare at him, waiting for him to proceed.

"Coach Burns, I have no doubt that what you've described for me probably took place just the way you say it did. She may have brushed against you with her leg, but that doesn't mean there was anything sexual in it. On the other hand, I don't think you'd come in here and lie about a thing as serious as this. But what you call 'sexual harassment' is more than likely Lucy just being Lucy, if you know what I mean … Now, I'm obligated to remind you that you can file an official complaint against Ms. Free in the form of a letter to Mr. Jones, our associate superintendent in charge of personnel. I'm sure you're familiar with Arthur Jones."

"Yes, I am."

"Once the charge is filed, Mr. Jones will interview both you and Ms. Free together to see how things stand between you. If, after talking with the both of you, he feels that the situation cannot be resolved amicably, he will make a recommendation to bring the matter before the School Board. You may want to seek legal representation at that time, but Mr. Burns, just a bit of personal advice; I'd strongly encourage you to settle this matter before it reaches the School Board. There are people on the board who have known Lucy Free since she was a student here some forty years ago, if you get my drift."

"Right. I understand what you're saying."

"I hope you do because Coach Goodson tells me you have a promising career ahead of you as a football coach. We'd like to see you spend it here at the Beach. Jerry can't coach forever, you know … Coach, just make sure you get on the right side of this kind of situation—don't mistake friendliness for a Friday night fling."

"I won't … There is one thing, Dr. Roberson, that is still troubling about this whole situation though."

"What's that?" Roberson says stubbing out another cigarette with visible annoyance.

"Her use of the word 'nigger' in referring to one of her library aides … her obvious racial prejudice."

"Mr. Burns," Roberson says leaning forward in his seat toward me, "let me give you a little history lesson about this area of the country. Now, first of all, you must understand I wasn't a resident here back then, but they tell me that in the late Forties right after the war, there was a sign at the Beach Gate someone had put up that read, 'Nigger, don't let the sun go down on you in Columbia Beach.' You see at that time, before the integration problem was solved in the 1960s, there were no blacks living in Columbia Beach. Most of the blacks who worked at the Beach as deckhands on fishing boats, or as kitchen help in the restaurants and casinos, or as maids at the hotels and motels on the Beach lived in a swampy area south of town in Westmoreland County known as 'The Swamp' … and because of that Beach residents derogatorily referred to them as 'swampers' just about as often as they called them 'niggers.' It's only been since Martin Luther King and the Civil Rights legislation of the Sixties that Blacks have been able to find housing at the Beach, particularly in the neighborhood surrounding Jackson Street, which as I'm sure you know has been—quite appropriately, I believe—changed to King Street. Are you with me, Coach?"

"Yes, I think I am. But please go on. What does this have to do with Ms. Free?"

"Well, as she will tell you if you ask her about it, all this racial prejudice happened in a time and place so dim and distant that degrees in library science at that time, including the one she was working on herself, were earned and awarded on the undergraduate level. Of course, nowadays, as you well know from your own research in this area, a degree or even a certification in library science must be accompanied by a master's degree."

"I understand that, Mr. Roberson. But with all due respect, sir, and maybe I'm just a little slow on the uptake, what does this have to do with her use of this racial epithet?"

"My point is," he says flicking ashes from his cigarette onto the glass-plated surface of his desk, "having been born and raised in this area, she grew up with certain attitudes toward blacks that, no doubt, were fostered by her family and embedded in her mind over a long period of time. For her to use the term 'nigger'—and I'm not condoning its use by her or any faculty member—was no more than a slip of the tongue, as far as I'm concerned. She was just slipping back into an earlier way of expressing herself without really thinking about what she was saying. In my judgment, neither you nor I should lose any sleep over the incident. Her use of this term wasn't in the presence of the student, was it, Coach? You were the only one who heard her?"

"That's true, as far as I know. But, Dr. Roberson, it's not just the use of this racial slur that's in question, is it? It says something about the person using it, and don't you think ..."

Before I can finish my thought, he cuts in brusquely, his eyes narrowing, "It's not your job to speculate on which faculty members are prejudiced and which are not. That's my worry, not yours, Coach. I'm the one who'll have to answer to the School Board if I allow a teacher onstaff to exhibit racial bias. As I indicated to you earlier in our conversation, I've talked to Ms. Free about this, and I intend to talk with her again following our conversation ... There's no doubt in my mind that once I speak to Lucy about this matter I'm sure it will never happen again," he says, flashing a tight smile. "And you can take that to the bank, as they say, Coach Burns," he says standing and extending his hand to me, giving me a quick pat on the back as he pumps my hand. "I appreciate you bringing these matters to my attention, Coach. We're certainly lucky to have someone like you on our staff. If you ever have another concern about how things are done here at the Beach, remember, my door is always open."

26

When I step outside the School Board office, I notice the wind off the river has picked up as it often does late in the afternoon here. It swirls around me, occasionally darting into the corners of the three-sided courtyard between the gym and the cafeteria that serves as a faculty parking lot, stirring up spent pieces of notebook paper and food wrappers—the usual debris from another day at Columbia Beach High School. There are only two vehicles in the lot—my VW wagon and Jerry's cherry red Custom van. The van, which Jerry purchased for $500 at the annual Columbia Beach Sheriff's Department's vehicle auction with a special dispensation from C.A.—It was a dealers-only auction—has seen better days. But this afternoon, so have I. At this particular moment, all I want to do is slip out of here unnoticed and head straight for Michelle's house. But as I quicken my step across the parking lot toward the Blue Bunny, the driver's side door of the van opens. Jerry leans out carrying a cardboard box bulging with papers under his arm.

"What's your hurry, son? Are you lookin' for me or is somebody after you?" Jerry asks out of the corner of his mouth.

I do an about face and head for him, "Actually, I was on my way to Michelle's for some dinner. Want to join us?"

"No, I wouldn't want to get in the middle of that," he says with a chuckle that dies quickly in his throat. Then, he makes a beeline for the school, as though he has got something pressing to do that does not include me. I stop and watch him for a minute wondering if he wants some company or not.

"How did your meeting with Robo go?" he tosses over his shoulder still walking toward the school.

"How 'd you know about that?" I start after him at a jog. When I catch up to him, he hands me the cardboard box so he can fish his keys out of his jacket pocket and open the gym door. He turns the key one way then back the other, all the while giving me the look of a man who's just reeled me in. Finally, the balky tumblers click.

"Gomer told me. Come down to my office and talk to me while I file this stuff," pointing a finger at the box I'm now saddled with.

"You'd be better off filing some of this stuff in the circular file, Coach. I don't see how you can find anything down here with all this clutter."

"Don't worry about me. I've got my own filing system. You name it and I can tell you what box it's in. Just try me."

"Jerry, I'd like to hang around and test your system, but it's been a long day and I need to get over to Michelle's and grab something to eat."

"Okay ... but before you leave tell me what Robo had to say."

I sit down facing Jerry across his desk and recount my meeting with Roberson as head down, squinting through a cracked pair of reading glasses, he listens while examining papers from the cardboard box I had carried in, separating them into piles. When I get to the part about Lucy's library science degree being an undergraduate one, he stops shuffling papers and looks up, "Hold up there, chief. Back up and run that by me again. Are you saying that Robo told you Loosey-Goosey only has a bachelor's degree in Library Science? Is that what you're saying?"

"That's what he told me ... that Lucy had said that all this racial prejudice stuff had taken place in the deep, dark, distant past when the library science degree she had been working on was on the undergraduate level—a bachelor of science, I believe."

"If she's teaching on a certificate with dust all over it," he fumes, "then why am I being forced to run down to VCU every Monday night to get certified in secondary administration? If she doesn't need a master's to run that library, then why do I need certification in administration just so I can hand out detention slips to tardy students? Tell me that, Spinach Man."

"I didn't know you were."

"What? Handing out detention slips? Or taking administration courses at VCU?"

"Taking courses."

"You didn't? Really? You didn't think I get to come down here, prop my feet up on my desk, put the NCAA Tournament game on the tube, and pretend I'm available to handle any disciplinary matter Gomer sends me for the price of an undergraduate degree did you? If that's what you're thinkin', you'd better think again. And while we're at it, Lucy better think about it, too. You have to have paid for an advanced degree if you want that kind of gig. And that's not the school system talkin', that's the state of Virginia, my friend."

"So, how's Lucy getting by with it?"

"I don't know, but I'm going to find out, that's for sure. I'll get Virginia to pull her personnel file on Monday. Then, we can determine whether Ms. Lucy Free's certification requires some updating."

"And if her certificate is not up to snuff, what then?"

"We'll have to find a board member who's willing to put it on the agenda for next month's board meeting … Charley Weatherly might be the man for the job. I owe him a favor, but then he owes my Daddy a couple, so one more on either side probably won't matter."

"You mean the Charley Weatherly who owns Little Vegas? He's on the School Board? That Charley Weatherly!" I exclaim in disbelief.

"Which Charley Weatherly did you think it was? Don't you read the newspaper?"

"*The Washington Post*, yes, but not *The Westmoreland Times.*"

"You better get on the ball then, Spinach Man, if you plan on staying around here for any length of time," he says standing up, shaking his head and slapping me playfully on the back.

"Now wait a minute. Don't go running off."

Jerry plants his right ass cheek on the side of his desk, folds his hands in front of him, and asks, "What else do you want to know?"

"Well, let's say, for starters that Lucy's teaching certificate is no longer valid; then, what would they do ... fire her?"

"No, no way. The most the School Board would be bound by state guidelines to do would be to insist that she go back to school and complete her master's in library science within an agreed upon time. But that could work in your favor, don't you see? To get rid of her, they wouldn't have to fire her; they'd just have to make getting her degree so difficult that she'd leave of her own accord. The other angle on this is that someone like Lucy in her early sixties might not want to put in the time running up and down the road in the middle of the night to Richmond or College Park just to hold onto a job she'll be retiring from in two or three years anyway. Not to mention the expense involved in tuition, books, and gas ... In addition, Lucy's been here a long time, you know; some of these newer board members might jump at the opportunity for a transfusion of new blood into the library—you know, reorganize it, bring in some new technology, revitalize it, turn it into a place the kids want to use. That's where you come in, Spinach Man. Have you looked into what schools around here offer certification programs in library science? If you haven't, you ought to."

"I plan to begin taking courses at VCU this summer. I already have my master's in English, so all I need to do is get my certification in library science."

"Yeah, I think you mentioned that to me one time. Well, get on the stick, man. Let Robo know about the course work you plan to take this summer; then, the blow of losing Lucy won't be so hard for him to take, if the School Board pushes her out the door. And, hey, forget about this sexual harassment and racial prejudice shit. According to what you've told me, you'll need a whole lot better evidence than what you have now to trip her up. All you have is basically your word against hers, isn't it? You don't have any witnesses, do you?"

I shake my head slowly, "No, you're right; it's just my word against hers."

"Okay, then, let me work on the certification angle. Let me see what Virginia can find in her personnel file, and I'll get back to you in a couple of days. Okay?"

"You've convinced me. I just hope Virginia can turn up something we can use … I appreciate your help on this one, Jer," I say extending my hand to him which he takes in a surprisingly flaccid grip. "I'm shoving off," I murmur, standing up. "I'm already late. Michelle doesn't like it when I'm late for supper."

"You sound like you're already married, slugger."

27

Despite the lateness of the hour, I take my time heading over to Michelle's. With everything that has transpired this afternoon, I feel wrung out and distracted. I tell myself I need a leisurely drive along the river to settle my nerves a bit before I see her. I know that not only will she be upset with me for not calling to tell her I am going to be late for supper, she'll want to know where I've been all this time. Then, I'll have to run back over the ground I have just covered with Robo and Jerry—something I'm not in the mood to do just yet. So, I swing down through town toward a triangular peninsula of land called the Point, bounded on one side by the Potomac and on the other by Monroe Bay. Once there, I turn onto a two-lane road skirting the river, offering from its elevated position above the water a panoramic view on my left of the Potomac all the way to the Maryland side. There's enough breeze out of the north to cloak the waves in white caps, sending a flotilla of dark clouds scudding across the river toward me like brooding thoughts. Even though it is early June, the wind has cooled the air enough to raise goose bumps on my bare arms. I close my window. Rain is on the way.

On the river side of the Point, there is a curious mixture of large Victorian era houses, gabled and peaked and fitted with widows' walks up high in front, and small flat-roofed cracker box motels painted in garish yellows, greens and purples, both huddling up to the edge of the road like two generations of a dysfunctional family. At the point of the triangle, where Monroe Bay empties into the Potomac, sits the Merry Mariner restaurant and bar amid a parking lot nearly full. It is the middle of the dinner hour. I check my watch. It is rapidly approaching 7:00 p.m..

I have dillydallied too long. Across the bay I can make out what I imagine are the lights of Michelle's bungalow sitting down low along the shore. At once an unsettling sensation of loss pervades me, and I am anxious to be there with her. The sky is darkening by the minute. So, I turn back to my right and wind along the bayside back toward the middle of town, trying to beat the approaching storm. The wind whips through the branches of the trees along Columbia Beach Boulevard, turning the leaves inside out. At the Beach Gate, the first rumblings of thunder chase me down Rte.205 toward the safe harbor of Michelle's abode.

"Is that you, Sugar?"

"Yes," I call through the screen door as I remove my shoes which have picked up some moisture on the way from the car to Michelle's front door.

"Why are you so late? It's after seven. The next time you're going to be this late," she scolds, "give me a call, *s'il vous plait.*"

"I'll try," I say, hesitating a moment before I enter, drinking in Michelle's loveliness as she stands at the kitchen counter with her back to me chopping vegetables for the stir fry she is preparing. Framed by the doorway and the light that bleeds out of the kitchen into the darkened living room, her blonde tresses and long shapely legs turn my thoughts to other appetites. Like a silent intruder, I steal up behind her and wrap my arms around her waist, cradling a breast in each hand, gauging her reaction. She does not resist. She even leans back into me momentarily as I kiss her neck, but then she pulls herself forward, refocusing her attention on the carrot she's slicing.

"Where have you been all this time?" she asks.

At that moment, I have no inkling of the firestorm my response will spark just as a minute or two before I had no way of knowing that this vision of Michelle standing at the kitchen counter with her back to me is the image of her my memory will preserve.

That night we fought insanely. We fought before supper, did not speak during supper, and resumed the fray after supper. What did we fight about? You might as well ask what didn't we fight about. Once I let her know that I'd been late because, first of all, I'd been talking to Robo in his office and, subsequently, with Jerry in his, discussing Lucy Free, Michelle wanted to know every word we had spoken on the subject. And so I told her. And when she heard the words that had passed across Roberson's desk and what was being plotted even at this late hour with Jerry and Virginia's help, she flew into a fit incandescent enough to melt metal or harden a heart. And when she finally caught me in the crosshairs of her fury, she fired all of her guns one after the other.

In Michelle's eyes, I was the one who had just sat back and let Lucy practice her own brand of hospitality without expressing a word of disapproval or warning, taking notes just as Jerry had told me to, giving her enough rope to hang herself with. ("I never gave her any encouragement," I protest. "Why did I need to have sex with a sixty-year-old woman? I had you. Besides, she was disgusting.")

According to Michelle, I was the one who had disliked Lucy from the first day I had set foot in the library despite all the help she had given me in becoming acclimated to library procedures. ("It wasn't her I disliked. It's what she did that I objected to. You remember the little incident with the lamp the first day I was in there with her? She's unprofessional; people like her have no business in education. Don't you see that?")

From Michelle's perspective, I was the one who wanted Lucy gone so that I could take over the Media Center and run it the way I wanted. ("I could care less about the Media Center. It's what takes place on the football field that matters to me. Sure, there are changes that need to be made in the Media Center—improvements in technology, weeding the collection, additions to the collection, above all a willingness to go the extra mile to help students access the information they need—all the things that Lucy never showed the least interest in. Even though the Media Center only ranks third on my list of priorities, (behind you and football) it will still be one hundred per cent better off with me running the show than with Lucy at the helm. You can't deny that!")

And finally, in a cut to the quick, I am the one who is never satisfied. No matter where I go, there's always something better just over the hill or around the bend. I am never happier than when I 'm warming my hands by the flames of a burning bridge. ("I have to admit there's nothing more appealing to me than a clean slate or a fresh sheet of paper—no reputation to live down, no hard feelings to get over, and no mistakes to try to rise above. I always look forward to starting fresh no matter where I'm coming from or where I'm going to.")

"So you are planning to leave, aren't you?" she sobs, throwing herself face down on the couch.

"Only if you come with me," I plead pulling her up, taking her in my arms, trying to kiss away her tears. "Come with me."

She presses her index finger to my lips and takes my hand in hers, leading me silently to her bedroom where we make love like two ship-wrecked survivors desperately holding onto the spar of our love. And after our energy is spent, she sends me home to my bed insisting that she has a 9:00 a.m. dentist appointment in Fredericksburg, so she will have no time to dally with me in the morning.

"Come by after lunch and we'll go for a bike ride around the Point or something," are her last words to me.

The next day when I arrive at her place around noon, I notice that her car is not in the driveway. Sensing nothing more than the thought that I must be early, I make my way to the front door only to find a folded piece of loose-leaf paper with my name on it scotch taped to the storm door. With a sinking feeling in my heart, I tear open the note. It hits me like a kick in the gut:

Dear Michael,

I know this is unexpected, but I've gone to my sister's in Georgia. I don't know if I'll be gone for a month or for the whole summer, but I've deliberately withheld her address and phone number. What I really need now is something you can't give me—time to think—so don't try to follow me. When I've sorted things out, I'll call you, I promise. I hope you realize that this is just as difficult for me as it is for you. If you're still at the Beach when I return, I'll know you still love me. But if you find another coaching job somewhere else this summer, I'll know there's still something more important to you than us.

Je t'aime

Michelle

28

Michelle's decision changed everything for me. Now there would be one fewer voice calling my name, one fewer kiss warming my lips, one fewer caress healing my heart, and one fewer reason to remain at the Beach this summer. Even if Robo put Lucy Free in mothballs for the rest of her natural life, that would not be enough to keep me at Columbia Beach HS for another year without Michelle. As sure as the water is deep, Michelle would sense that I was behind Lucy's demise and would inevitably lose faith in me. And I would not be able to remain at the Beach if she weren't on my side. Besides, I was convinced there was still coaching to do, football to be played, and glory to be won down the road.

It is remarkable how hard it is to get where you want to go and how easy it is to leave where you don't want to be. Unfortunately, in my case, I am more familiar with the latter than the former. On the day following Michelle's departure, I spent a couple of hours packing my clothes into the back of the Bunny; typing out a letter of resignation; and saying my good-byes to Whitey, Bear, Jonathan, and Rondell, explaining that my football dreams were calling me to bigger and better things, perhaps back in North Carolina, without ever mentioning that I had no idea where I was going or what I was headed for.

Strangely enough, I relished the thunderstruck look on each of their faces when I informed them of my intention. Of course, the first words out of their mouths after hearing of my decision were what about Michelle? Was she going with me? What were her plans? All I could tell them was that Michelle had been unexpectedly called away to her sister's in Georgia, that she might be gone for a month or more, and that we would be in touch with each other soon, intimating that her swift departure was family-related so that I wouldn't have to go into the sticky details of what was actually going on between us.

I was packed and ready to go, but I had one more stop to make before shoving off. I found Jerry in his office wearing his favorite Carolina T-shirt, which read, "If God is not a Tar Heel, then why is the sky Carolina blue?" and his red, white, and blue Eagles baseball cap counting last week's take from the soft drink and Nab machines stationed strategically around campus to maximize their profitability. Having been fewer than seventy-two hours since we had both been sitting at this same desk plotting Lucy's downfall, the news of my departure had caught him off guard. All he seemed able to do was to keep repeating what a big part of the team's success this year I had been and what had he done to run me off. I tried to reassure him that he was in no way responsible for my leaving, offering a detailed explanation of the situation with Michelle and how I was seeking a coaching situation that would allow me to develop my own coaching philosophy. Never mentioning, all the while, why I couldn't do that at the Beach.

"It sounds to me like you're looking for a head coaching job," he said.

"Yes, that's what I have in mind."

"Wouldn't it make more sense to hang onto the position you have here until you can find a head-coaching job? If that's what you want, I'll help you any way I can."

"You're probably right, but even if I don't get a head job right off the bat, maybe a couple of years with a AAA or a AAAA program might better prepare me to be a head coach."

"Okay," he says holding up his hands as though I were pointing a gun at him, "I understand what you're saying. Columbia Beach is not exactly a big time high school football program. But we have had some success here despite our size. And I'm not planning on cashing in my chips anytime soon. I've still got a good ten years left in coaching. But if you hang around long enough, there'll be a head coaching opening here one day."

"You're probably right, but with the way things are with Michelle and the situation in the library, a fresh start somewhere else may be my best bet."

"You sound like you've pretty much set your sails in that direction, Spinach Man. Am I right? Huh?" he asks punctuating his question with a soft punch to my right shoulder.

"Yes, you are."

"Before you run, let me put in one call to this fella I know," Jerry says, cradling the receiver with his shoulder while punching in the number. "How do you feel about North Carolina?"

"Good. I'm pretty sure I'm still certified there."

After making a couple of calls, Jerry was able to track down an old coaching buddy from his days as the head coach at Nixon HS across the river in Maryland—Daryl Fields. Coach Fields was now the head coach at Richland High School in Rockingham, NC, a powerhouse program that had won the State AAAA championship the last two years running. Despite the fact that Coach Fields had eight coaches including himself on staff, he did have an opening for a varsity assistant to coach the running backs and an offensive play caller for the JV program—excellent preparation for someone interested in a head coaching job down the road. On the academic end, Richland had an opening for an instructor in its remedial English program. It sounded like a good fit, given my background in English. So, we scheduled an interview for the end of the week. With Jerry and Daryl's prior relationship plus Jerry's willingness to go the extra mile on my behalf, I felt like a shoe-in for the position.

After the handshakes and hugs were exchanged and the gratitude freely expressed, particularly from my side after what Jerry had just done for me, all that was left was for me to drop my letter of resignation into Jerry's outstretched palm and say good-bye. "Don't be a stranger," were his last words to me in spite of the fact that Richland County was set among the Sandhills of North Carolina many miles distant from Columbia Beach.

So, I headed out—just the Blue Bunny and me cut loose from our moorings, drifting to who-knows-what on the tide of time and circumstance once again. Speeding out of town past the trailers and the one-story brick duplexes, I had a mental flash of Michelle standing in her kitchen with her back turned toward me, framed by the kitchen doorway and the fading sunlight, chopping vegetables for our dinner. *"Would we ever share another meal together?" I wondered.* As I approached the curve on 205 where it swoops down like a seabird to the river's edge, I saw the "Paradise on the Potomac" sign in my rear view. For a moment, my chin began to quiver and my eyes welled up. Then, it was gone from view and I was on the road heading south with tears staining my cheeks.

29

So down the gypsy highway I went—where all are brothers and all are strangers, where no sooner is your goal in sight than it recedes at the speed of light, where just when you begin to know who you are you become a stranger to yourself.

Never heard to use any expression stronger than "bull crap" on the practice field or even in the relative privacy of the coaches' office, Coach Daryl Fields was the most good-natured coach I'd ever been around. But it wasn't his geniality alone that brought him success; it was his energy and thoroughgoing knowledge of the game that placed him a step above any other coach I had ever worked for—before or since. Starting fresh, without any scrapes, scratches, or smudges on my slate, I learned more about coaching football during my three years under Coach Fields than I had in all my previous years of coaching combined. By my third year at Richland Senior, Coach Fields had rewarded my loyalty to the program by elevating me to offensive coordinator for the varsity. More importantly, we had added two more AAAA State Championship trophies to the school's athletic trophy case. By the end of my third season at Richland Senior HS, in the wake of a runner-up finish to Charlotte Independence in the state championship game, I felt that the organizational and leadership skills I had learned from Coach Fields had prepared me well. I was ready for my first head-coaching job. So, when Clifton High School, a small I-A school in Onslow County, offered me its head position, I jumped at it without a thought to what I might be getting into.

Clifton, located at the lower coastal end of the county, just south of Camp Lejeune and the New River, was chiefly populated by watermen and their sons, with just enough poor blacks situated farther inland in Maple Hill to make for a lethal mixture of football talent or volatile racial division—or both. Like Columbia Beach, Clifton's economy fed off its proximity to the water, but unlike the Beach, where the majority of blacks and whites rubbed elbows on a daily basis, cooling any racial differences, the geographic separation of the races in this part of Onslow County fed their fears and fanned the flames of racial prejudice. So, I learned quickly to be careful to give my white players as much ink in the local newspaper as I gave the blacks after a game, or I would have an angry white parent bending my ear on Monday morning.

Things ran smoothly at first. Keeping in mind Coach Fields' gentle leadership, I put my arm around the players' shoulders and spoke softly to them when they made a mistake, and I patted them on the butt and clapped my hands when they succeeded. Uppermost in my mind was the thought that I would only win them over with trust, not intimidation. Still, we lost our first game to Woodson Academy, 21-0, but when I put the blame on my shoulders for not doing a good job of preparing them, they seemed to rally around me by working their butts off in preparation for our next opponent, Drummond HS. All week long, I promised them that their hard work would pay off, and they made a prophet of me on Friday night by whipping the Dragons, 14-7, at home. We kept the momentum rolling the following week at Deep Run, defeating a larger Mustang squad, 28-7, in a driving rainstorm behind the determined running of David Samuels, our black slot back, whom I had nicknamed "Lightning in a Bottle." On the bus ride back to Clifton, the players chanted, "David, David, David" and then "Burns, Burns, Burns" until they fell asleep, finally succumbing to the cool air and fatigue. All the coaches, including myself, looked at each other with smiles that wouldn't wipe off our faces, allowing ourselves to believe, after only three games, that we were on our way now.

We worked some of our recent magic for the home crowd at Bulldog Field the following Friday night, roaring back from a 20-7 halftime deficit to defeat Magnolia HS, 31-20. I was so energized by our comeback victory that I nearly sprinted across the field at the final whistle just to ask the Magnolia coach if he'd ever witnessed a better high school football game. He must have thought I was having some fun at his expense because he just shook my hand and kept on walking. In the wake of our rousing victory, everyone—players, coaches, parents, teachers, and administrators—was primed for Homecoming against archrival Hampstead the next week and even began talking playoffs for the Bulldogs for the first time in years. What no one could know, including myself, was that the victory over Magnolia would be the high water mark of our season—we would not taste victory again that year.

Looking back on it now, about the middle of Homecoming week was when I first had the feeling that the foundation was beginning to move around underneath me in the dark void that, I see now, was always there beneath my feet. It started with a phone call midweek from the parent of some player whose name I've long forgotten complaining about how I was giving too much playing time to the black players and not enough to the white players like his son. And, furthermore, that he wasn't the only one in the community who was upset about my 'nigger-lovin' ways." That was when I should have loosened my hold on the telephone and set the receiver gently back in its cradle. I see that now, but I didn't see it then. So, when I felt all the good that we had accomplished up until then start to slide away, I tightened my grip on that receiver as though that poor Cracker were trying to steal something from me that I knew was mine. So, I gave him a tongue lashing on the subject of racism in the South that I would later discover had reverberated form Sneads Ferry to Surf City on the coast and to Maple Hill and back.

From that moment on, everything started to slip away like a ship sinking in a sickening spiral, sucking all of us down with it. First, we lost the game to Hampstead on a last second field goal, 10-7. Then, on Monday morning, we lost our co-captain and all-conference linebacker, Dennis Frazier, when his grandfather told him to turn in his equipment because he didn't want him playing for some "nigger-lovin' Yankee coach" any longer. Then, I lost my temper later in the week and sent two players packing for clowning around at practice, yelling at them, "You ain't shit," as they left the practice field spewing shoulder pads, helmets, arm pads, and obscenities. What it all came down to was I lost my cool, I lost my poise, I lost control, I lost my players, and then I lost my way.

Every week we lost by a larger margin—twenty points, thirty points, forty points—than the week before. Who did I think I was—railing at officials, cussing players, calling timeouts so I could yell and scream at rival coaches from the middle of the playing field? I knew who I was becoming, but it was as if the train was a-rolling and I couldn't stop it. It was out of my hands now. I'd lost sight of everything Daryl Fields had taught me. I had become Jerry. When things had gotten tough, instead of believing in myself and having faith in my players, I had reverted back to the in-your-face, confrontational style of coaching I'd seen produce results before—Jerry's style. Now I couldn't help remembering Michelle's promise over crabs to keep me from falling into that trap. If she had been there with me, none of this would have happened. I was sure of that.

It didn't take long to wear out my welcome. That season was my first and last as head coach of the Clifton Bulldogs. In the coaching profession, bad news travels even farther and faster than good, so the news of my self-destruction seemed to follow me everywhere I went. I spent the next six years as an assistant coach, drifting from one school system to another in North Carolina and Virginia—Pender Co., Transylvania Co., Fauquier Co.—waiting for another shot as a head coach, a shot that seemed as if it would never come again.

On the off-chance that something good might turn up, I even tried to contact Onancock High School in the hope that turning back to the source of my once bright and shining coaching vision would revitalize my career. But it was not to be. When I telephoned the School Board office in Accomack County, (VA) a secretary whose snappish tone of voice sounded as if she'd taken one too many phone calls on the subject of Onancock HS transferred me to the county technology center. Then, a gentler voice with a Yankee accent filled the receiver explaining that the school had become the Accomack County Center for Technology five years ago. I was stunned. Onancock had suddenly disappeared like an old friend who had passed away while I was looking the other way. I hesitated a minute and then asked the kindly voice what had become of the school's former head football coach.

"Coach Patwell? Is that who you mean? He passed away not too long ago while working in his garden one Sunday afternoon. It's been about two years, I'd say, since he passed."

"What happened? Heart attack?"

"No, I believe he had a stroke."

"I'm sorry to hear that. He was a great coach."

"Yes, everyone in the community loved him … especially his players. Did you know Coach Patwell very well?"

"I knew of him, ma'am. I only knew of him. Thanks for your help," I said as I hung up the phone, feeling as though a page had been ripped from my book of days with his passing. Later that evening as I gazed out the living room window of my nearly bare one-bedroom apartment, I saw in my mind's eye Michelle standing with her back to me preparing dinner silhouetted by the evening sun pouring through the kitchen window and knew the day was growing late.

30

It is a sunny Monday morning in mid-June, and I am traveling east on Route 3 from Fauquier County to make a 2:00 p.m. meeting with Jerry and the new superintendent of Columbia Beach Schools, Dr. Anne Colson. For some inexplicable reason (nerves, I guess), I get confused coming through Falmouth (on a road I have driven a thousand times) and turn left on Route 218, the so-called "backdoor" to the Beach, a way I have rarely traveled before. I find myself winding along a narrow two-lane road bordered on both sides by thick vegetation that has crawled over the shoulder of the road like hair curling over a ragged shirt collar. Suddenly, a wave of apprehension sweeps through me as I imagine that just around the next bend the road will dead end and the Blue Bunny and I will be swallowed by a morass of kudzu never to be found again—not to mention missing what could be the most important appointment of my coaching career.

When I heard Jerry's voice on the other end of the line on Friday afternoon, the sound of it shot through me like an old, familiar song. He never engaged in small talk, at least not on the telephone; when he called, something was up. And true to form, what he had to say changed the way I had been looking at the day. He was retiring as head football coach at the Beach; though, he planned to stay on as athletic director. Was I interested in the job? Could I come down on Monday, interview with Dr. Colson (the Beach was between principals again), and sign the contract?

"Just like that?"

"Just like that."

When Jerry wanted something done, he worked quickly.

I can hardly sleep a wink the whole weekend waiting for Monday to arrive. I set sail early that morning; not only am I in a lather to sign the necessary papers, there is someone I want to talk to before I sit down with Jerry and Dr. Colson. But now one wrong turn has me nervous. Have I ever been on this road before? Does it actually lead to the Beach? Where does it intersect 205? I've forgotten the place. My thoughts are spinning, putting me on edge, until I cross Route 301 above the Naval Surface Weapons Center at Dahlgren. Once there, I get my bearings; I set a short course for the junction of 218 and 205 just above Potomac Beach. I just pray that I will have enough time to find Michelle before I am scheduled to meet with Jerry and Dr. Colson.

At some point during that fateful summer of 1979, while Michelle was still at her sister's, she must have gotten wind of my departure from the Beach to points south. Then, there ensued a virtual torrent of letters and telephone calls (she must have gotten my number from Jerry) imploring me beseeching me to reconsider, that it was not too late to return. I tried to keep up, really I did. But eventually I realized that we had about as much chance of carrying on a relationship at long distance as a penguin has of flying. So, with football practice at Richland set to begin on the first day of August, I began letting my responses to Michelle's missives slide—one week, two weeks, three weeks, a month. Often I found myself fishing her last letter out of my desk, reading it again for the umpteenth time, and then sitting there staring at it waiting for some words to come. But it just became harder to find something to say to her other than talking about what was taking place on the football field—stuff I was sure she didn't want to hear. So, around the middle of the season when her torrent had shrunk to a trickle, I stopped answering her letters altogether. With the chances of me ever returning to the Beach seeming to be slim to none, I knew, as I'm sure

Michelle did too, that there was no point in drawing out a situation that appeared more hopeless with each passing week. We could pretend all we wanted, but we both knew it was better this way.

By the time I had been hired as an assistant coach by Fauquier County two years ago, our communication had dwindled to nothing more than a card at Christmas. Forget her, though, I never could. I just wonder if she feels the same way as I speed down 205, past the "Paradise on the Potomac" sign, toward the Beach. It is only a little after eleven in the morning. I still have time to find her before my meeting at two o'clock.

I cup my hands around my eyes and press them against the windowpane of the front door, dispelling reflections, as I peer into the murky interior. But all it tells me is exactly what the two pollen-covered metal porch chairs turned upside down on the porch already have told me—no one is occupying what used to be Michelle's bungalow on Monroe Bay, least of all Michelle.

"Who ya' lookin' for?" a raspy voice calls out from behind, startling me. I wheel around coming face to face with one of the denizens of the Beach, a mournful waterman looking as if his boat has sunk. He's wearing a pair of stained khakis, a discolored thermal undershirt with the sleeves cut off which barely covers his swollen beer belly, and a white "Bass Fishing" baseball cap pulled down so low on his forehead that the brim obscures most of his face except his thick, salt-and-pepper moustache. He takes a drag off the de rigueur cigarette, coughs, then spits through the handful of teeth he still has and adds sticking out his hand, "I'm Boyd McCall. Can I help you?"

I reach out and take it, but before I can tell him who I am looking for, he starts right in, "I've lived across the street from this house for near onto thirty years now," gesturing with his cigarette back behind himself at his small white, siding-covered ranch. "I was here when they built it back in '63, and I've seen them come and go. Every single one of them."

"I'm Michael Burns. Maybe you remember me. I used to coach football at the high school under Jerry Goodson back about ten years ago." I pause to see if something will click in his mind. It doesn't.

"Can't say as I do … how long did you coach here, son?"

"One year."

"That's all? One year! There's no way in hell I'd remember someone who just coached one year here at the Beach." he spits again. "But I do know of this Jerry Goodson fella. He's C.A.'s son, ain't he?"

"You're right about that, Mr. McCall."

"Huh?"

"I say you're right about Jerry Goodson," raising my voice a few decibels to make myself heard. "He's the son of C.A. Goodson."

"Yeah, I know … who you lookin' for? Jerry? He don't live out this way. He lives over off 205, I believe."

"I know where Jerry lives," cutting him off in frustration. "I'm looking for a woman by the name of Michelle Lemonde—French teacher at the high school. She was probably the last person to occupy this house. Do you know who I mean?"

"Tall, blonde-haired woman? That the one?"

"Yes. It looks like she's moved, though. You don't happen to know where she moved to, do you?"

"Yeah, I do … she told my wife she was moving over to the Point. Do you know where that is, young fella?" he grins resting a hand crusty with callous on my shoulder.

"Yes, I think I know where the Point is. I used to live here ten years ago. It hasn't moved in ten years has it?" I respond testily as I feel time starting to slip away from me. "Do you happen to know the address over there where she moved to, Mr. McCall? There must be a hundred houses on the Point."

"No … but I can go check with Trudi. She might know. She's my wife, you see," he says turning to go back to his house.

He returns a few minutes later with Trudi in tow—a short, barrel-shaped woman with her hair the color of orange marmalade pulled back in a bun and a smile crinkled with crows feet around her eyes.

"Coach Burns, this is my wife Trudi."

But before I can get a word out, she says with a smile, "Boyd here says you're looking for Michelle. Are you *the* Michael Burns? The one she talks about who used to be a coach up at the school?"

"I am," I say returning her smile. "I'm glad to hear she still mentions me … I hope she speaks well of me."

"She does on occasion, but at other times not so well. It depends on when you catch her."

"Well, that's what I'm trying to do right now is catch up with her. Do you know where on the Point she has moved to?"

"No, I don't. I wish I did. I don't think she ever gave me her new address, or maybe she did and I just don't recall it. At my age, Mr. Burns, it's hard to keep everything in my mind … I wish I could help you."

"It's Coach Burns, Trudi, not Mr. Burns," Boyd interjects. "My wife's sixty-seven years old, Coach Burns. Of course, I'm a little older than her. Just turned seventy in January. But I don't have no trouble remembering things, Coach. Like Trudi here does."

"Well, aren't you something," she bristles putting her hands on her hips and glaring at him through narrowed eyes the way Michelle would do when she was angry with me.

Returning her glare and then turning back to me, McCall asks, "Coach, did you say that the Lemonde woman was French? 'Cause if she is, she sure don't have a French accent."

"She's not French, you ninny; she teaches French," Trudi booms with a laugh.

"She could be both," Boyd offers sheepishly.

"But she's not, silly," Trudi insists

"She's right, Mr. McCall." I pause pondering the situation for a moment. Who could I call without letting Jerry know that I'm in town early? I wonder. Then, it hits me. The School Board office has got to have her new address. How else could they send out her paycheck? I'll call Jerry's wife Virginia; she'll know it. I'll just have to swear her to secrecy until I find Michelle and have a chance to talk with her.

"Could I ask a favor of you? Could I use your phone?"

I am on my way back across town toward the Point with Michelle in mind when something—either force of habit or blind coincidence—tells me to take the Douglas Avenue shortcut, which skirts the old school building. As I drive past the school, I catch a glimpse of something that causes me to take a left at the next stop sign and drive around the block instead of following Douglas to the Point. It's the solitary form of a stocky black man pushing the trash around in front of the school entrance with a broom. He's sporting a white sweatshirt with the arms cut out; red, white, and blue Eagles' basketball shorts with boxers hanging out below them; and a now-out-of-style box haircut.

On my first time around the block, he looks up at me from his sweeping but doesn't return my wave. On my second time around, I glide to a stop in front of the school and motion for him to come over. He approaches haltingly.

"Hey, Flip," I say extending my hand toward him.

He shakes it limply. "Hey, Coach."

"Good to see you. It's been a long time."

"I know," he says looking away, hiding a smile.

"You working for the school now?"

"Yeah."

"That's good. I'm happy for you."

"It's a job."

"Yeah, well, we'll be working together then."

"How do you mean?"

"I've been offered the head coaching job here at the Beach."

Flip's eyes light up when he hears this. "You takin' Goodson's job?"

"Well, he's retiring and he asked me if I was interested in the job …"

"Coach, you don't want to be comin' to this dump of a place."

"It's a job, isn't it?"

We both smile at this.

"I wish you had some eligibility left," I joke. "I could really use you."

"Naw, Coach, my football days are long gone. You know that."

"Yeah, I know it. I was just teasing you. Listen … maybe you can help me out some on Friday night. What do you say?"

"At the game? I'd like that. But I couldn't help out after school at practice. I don't get off work 'til five or sometimes five-thirty."

"I got you. We'll talk about it. Right now I'm on my way over to Mlle. Lemond's house."

"The French teacher?"

"Yes."

"Are you and her still talkin'?"

"That's what I want to find out, Flip. She's the main reason I'm thinking about coming back here."

"You know you comin' back here, Coach. Don't be tellin' no lies now," he says smiling genuinely for the first time. "You wouldn't be here right now if you weren't comin' back."

"You're probably right, Flip ... well, look, I've got to run. I want to see Mlle. Lemond before I interview at two. Take care, now. I'll be looking for you," I say as we grasp each other's hand in a soul grip.

"Be cool, Coach," he reminds me as I pull away from the curb.

I crawl past the white cottage on Parker Place two times before I finally grind to a halt on the gravel in front of her house. There's a red Honda parked in the driveway bearing a license plate that reads "BON VOYAG." As I approach the house, a figure materializes as a silhouette behind the screen door, leaning into the light with her forearms resting on the doorframe.

"Hello, stranger," she says, her salutation spilling evenly out of the shadows, "It's been a long time."

"Yes, it has. It really has."

For a moment, the screen door stands between us like the expanse of river that stretches from the Maryland to the Virginia side—dark, uncertain, and unfathomable—then, it swings wide. Except for a little more fullness in her figure, Michelle is still the same beautiful woman I used to know. I want to take her in my arms and hug her, but the miles and the years between us hold me back. So, I hesitate, waiting to see if she'll make the first move. She doesn't.

"Make yourself comfortable," she says motioning to a large easy chair. "Would you like something to drink?"

"Water will be fine. How did you know I was coming? Did Virginia call you?" I call out as she heads for the kitchen.

"No, Virginia didn't call me, but I did know you were coming. I ran into Jerry up at school last week. He mentioned to me that he was giving up the football and that he'd contacted you about the job. I knew you were coming down to interview; I just didn't know what day … I probably shouldn't tell you this, but all this week every time I heard a car go by I ran to the door to see if it was the Blue Bunny. I guess I just got lucky today," she says entering from the kitchen with a glass of water and a coy smile on her face. Still, we do not touch as she takes a seat on the couch opposite me.

"When's your interview?"

"Two o'clock … it's not really an interview. It's more or less a formality. Jerry's already offered me the job, and Dr. Colson will go along with his recommendation, or so I'm led to believe. I really just want to get some things settled in my mind before I sign the contract."

"Is that why you came here first?"

"Yes … you could say that."

"Same old Michael—everything still has to be just so before you're willing to commit, doesn't it?"

"Not everything … just one thing," I say as I lean forward in my chair toward her, extending a hand, hoping she'll put hers in mine, when the back door abruptly opens and slams shut.

"Mom," a child's voice cries from the kitchen, "Sparky won't give me back the ball."

"Come here for a minute. There's someone here I want you to meet," Michelle calls ignoring my inquiring eyes.

A tanned, sturdy-legged boy of nine or ten enters the room with a frown on his face beneath a tousled head of curly blonde hair. For a few moments, I examine the frustration and irritation playing across the child's face without saying a word; then, I look toward Michelle for some sort of explanation. But her eyes betray nothing except concern for him.

"Mitchell," she says, encircling him with her arms and kissing his cheek, "this is Coach Burns, an old friend of Mommy's."

"Hi … Mom, Sparky keeps taking the T-ball. Every time I hit the ball she takes it and won't give it back to me. Now, she's chewing on it out in the backyard."

"Well, we'll have to do something about that. How about if I bring Sparky inside while you hit the T-ball and I talk with Coach Burns. All right?"

"Okay," he says with a smile returning to his face.

Michelle and Mitchell depart to collect Sparky and the ball from the backyard while I recline in the easy chair in shock.

When Michelle returns, she's followed by Sparky, a medium-sized terrier mix with a curly black coat of hair, who flops down on her stomach at Michelle's feet, panting heavily, with her back legs splayed out flat. She then begins to drag herself across the carpet using only her front paws. Temporarily transfixed by this unusual maneuver, I watch speechless. Before I can begin to speak, Michelle, sensing my confusion over Mitchell, begins, "Michael, don't"—But I cut her off.

"Why didn't you tell me, Michelle? How could you have kept something like this from me?" my voice rising in irritation.

"What do you mean?

"You know damn well what I mean. Any fool can see that he's mine. I can't believe you never let me know."

"I couldn't have let you know something I didn't know myself until after you'd left. You know, if you hadn't been in such a hurry to find your coaching dream job, you might have been around when I found out I was pregnant."

"Maybe … but I don't see how you could have gotten pregnant in the first place. You were on the Pill."

"I went off the Pill that spring before you left the Beach."

"Why did you do that? You never told me you were going off the Pill. What were you using?"

"Nothing—I just went off the Pill."

"What in the hell were you thinking?"

"I could sense that you were inching toward leaving," she says with tears welling up in her eyes. "I was in love with you. I had to try to do something to make you stay. The only problem was even though I had gone off the Pill that spring, I didn't find out I was pregnant until some time in June. By that time, I was in Georgia and you were down in North Carolina coaching football."

"So, what you're telling me is you planned to get pregnant in order to get me to stay at the Beach, but it didn't work out. Right? What I don't understand, Michelle, is once you knew you were pregnant why you didn't let me know? We were still in contact with each other on a regular basis then. Why didn't you tell me?"

"Because I knew you were out there trying to find your dream," now the tears begin to run down her cheeks. "And I knew you'd resent me if you thought I was trying to blackmail you into coming back to the Beach … and to me. I couldn't do it. I knew I'd just have to wait and let your football wanderings run their course."

"Till I came back to the Beach, you mean?"

"Yes … something like that," she says, a sob catching in her voice.

"You were kind of taking a big chance there, weren't you? I mean there was no guarantee that I'd ever come back to the Beach. What if I'd have found what I was looking for at another school a long way from here? And not only that, but how did you know that if I did return, I'd feel the same way about you as I once did?" I ask reaching out and grasping her hand—the soft warm little-girl hand that used to slide so easily into mine.

"I didn't … I was just hoping," she says giving my hand a squeeze.

"Ten years is a long time to hope."

"It's a long time … but maybe not too long," she whispers, wiping the tears from her cheeks with her free hand. "Michael, I don't want to give you the wrong impression. I haven't been sitting here in Columbia Beach for the past ten years just waiting for you to come back because that's not true. I've taken my lovers and had my flings and suffered about an equal number of heartaches … plus one, counting you. Believe me, I've put you out of my mind a hundred times these past ten years, but I've never been able to forget you and what we had together, particularly with Mitchell here to raise."

"Michelle, I can't deny that the whole way down today from Fauquier I kept telling myself that you'd be as glad to see me as I am to see you, even after all this time. At least, that's what I hoped. I just didn't expect to find a ready-made family waiting for me."

"I know."

"But everything is going to be all right now. I'm here, you're here, and Mitchell's here. That's all that matters now. If there were ever any doubts in my mind about coming back to the Beach, they're gone now. I'm here to stay and be with you and Mitchell as long as you'll have me," I say cupping her face in my hands and kissing her softly on the lips. "Does he know who I am?"

"No, all I've told him is that his father used to teach here, but he decided he didn't like it at Columbia Beach and left. He's teaching down in North Carolina now. His Mommy didn't want to leave the Beach so she stayed."

"Does he believe that?"

"Why shouldn't he? It's the truth," she says, smiling and brushing her tears away at the same time.

"You're right, except for the North Carolina part. I've actually been working at Fauquier County HS for the past two years. Let me go tell him," I say rising from my chair.

"No, let him play. I'll make some sandwiches. We'll talk about it over lunch … like a family."

"That's a good idea."

All at once our eyes meet, her smile drawing me to her like an inexorable tide of years past and years to come, drawing me into deeper water—water much deeper than any I ever dreamed I had traveled in before. So, we loosen the lines and cast off—the three of us—setting sail with the wind at our backs on the warm and gentle waters of the river carrying us and a flotilla of a thousand dancing waves along on our journey together to the dark waters where the ships set sail.

Epilogue

While adjusting to Coach Burns' coaching style—a style based on trust and partnership—the Columbia Beach Eagles lose their first five games of the 1988 football season. However, after finally adapting to Coach Burns' coaching philosophy, they win their five remaining games, ending up the season with a break even record. Coach Michael Burns and Michelle Lemonde are married following the 1988 season. Their ten-year-old son Mitchell serves as the ring bearer at the ceremony.

978-0-595-42192-3
0-595-42192-X

Printed in the United States
74685LV00003B/158

9 780595 421923